Blasius Powentz †1563
mercenary soldier

Paulke Powentz †1599
tradesman

Hans Peter
Powensen
(Scand. line)

Rochus Powentz
stable-groom

Ivan Pavlovich
Povenzov
(Russ. line)

Ferry Baron Powenzl
(Viennese line)

Yadam Povenski
(Pol. line)

Bogumil Pwnc
(Czech. line)

Melchior Powenz *1866 †?
beggar

THE POWENZ PACK

THE POWENZ PACK

One Family's Chronicle

The definitive edition,
based on posthumous documents
and the most recent research data,
together with prefatory remarks
by the former mayor of the town of Moessel,
Dr. Max Dattel,
and prepared for the general public

by
Ernst Penzoldt
Curator

Translated from the German by
John E. Woods

FROMM INTERNATIONAL PUBLISHING CORPORATION

NEW YORK, NEW YORK

Originally published in 1939 as *Die Powenzbande*
Copyright © 1939, S. Fischer Verlag, Berlin and
1977, Suhrkamp Verlag, Frankfurt am Main

Translation Copyright © 1982 by Fromm International Publishing
Corporation, New York, N. Y.

Printed in the United States of America

First U. S. Edition

Library of Congress Cataloging in Publication Data

Penzoldt, Ernst, 1892–1955.
The Powenz pack.
Translation of: Die Powenzbande.   I. Title.
PT2631.E42P6513   1982   833′.912   81-22169
ISBN 0-88064-002-2   AACR2

THE POWENZ PACK

CONTENTS

Book of Hope

Book of Tribulations

Book of Edification

Baltus Powenz
Last known photograph

FOREWORD

To understand all things is to conceive all things.
—Baltus Powenz, Pedagogical Writings

Moessel on the Maar is a town wrapped in Powenzian legend. Its inhabitants are even now preparing for a solemn celebration marking the eighty-eighth birthday of Moessel's greatest son, Baltus Powenz. On the occasion of this great event, I, in my capacity as Moessel's mayor emeritus, have been accorded the high honor of prefacing a few well-tempered words to the jubilee edition of the biography of our (to our sorrow) late fellow citizen.

The author of these lines had the good fortune in life of having been intimately connected with the untimely deceased. The author may also take some modest credit in having played an initiatory role both in the founding of the Powenz Society and in the erection of the Baltus Powenz Monument, the latter providing our town a stately ornament for all time to come. Philatelists will also be gratified to learn of the issue of a special commemorative stamp bearing the countenance of this celebrated man. Faithfulness repaid with faithfulness!

The good relationship now extant between the worthy Powenz family and the town's inhabitants was troubled but briefly by certain petty misunderstandings that were then exaggerated through the ignorance and impotence of certain unscrupulous mischief-makers. The current rapid growth of tourism in our dear Moessel is due solely to the work of one man, Baltus Powenz—and to providence, of course. Today we may proudly say: "He was one of us."

This present edition of *The Powenz Pack* (the customary name given the family by the local population, though in jest and with no offense intended) has received my most energetic support. It was the earnest desire of the editorial committee (among whom are to be found the most renowned Powenz scholars) that the text be brought into accord with the latest research data available to them, while at the same time care be taken not essentially to alter the story of the life-affirming, heartwarming exploits that have now become a part of history, ineradicably engraved in the memory of the citizens of Moessel—even when certain of those exploits may not be historically verifiable. Such legendary accounts often contain more historical truth than mere sober facts. On the other hand, a respect for the feelings both of the bereaved family—especially for the widow who is now well advanced in years—

and of many readers has resulted in several emendations and omissions. The layman may choose merely to glance over the notes and appendices, since these have been included primarily for the specialist.

Max Dattel
Mayor Emeritus
President of the Powenz Society
Patron of the Monument Association
and Chairman of the Board of Directors
of Bad Heinrichsbrunn, Ltd.

BOOK OF HOPE

Man is but a shadow's dream.

—Pindar

Chapter One

In which a star falls from the sky
and dispatches the hero of our story

In a list of the most singular ways to die, one ought to include, I think, death by falling meteor, or put another way, being struck down by a stone hurled out from eternity; and it is understandable that the tale of a man thus slain should be taken up, his earthly adventures sung and his name made magic in the memory of his posterity—and just so did Baltus Powenz meet his death in our own day and before my very eyes.

Toward evening I had gone out for a little ride on the outskirts of town, and as often happened I met up with the eccentric old man; he spoke loudly to himself (or to God) and gesticulated furiously with both hands. He wore his old brown and gray check inverness and was, as usual, inebriated. He staggered a bit, but with dignity. And I saw a flame shoot down with a crack of thunder out of the starry sky, striking the old man as he wandered about bareheaded and unsuspecting. And its fire devoured him whole.

Gravely disquieted, I first calmed my horse

3

and then rode up closer. I discovered nothing but the blue smoke of his ashes borne peacefully on the woodland air, while around the black crater the grass went on smoldering and glimmering for some time.

This strange accident occurred not far from the remarkable house that old Powenz had built near the Moessel city line, though at the legally prescribed distance from it—that he had built, one might say, with his own hands in defiance and derision of the citizens who had driven him from their midst. For he had ever lived in conflict with the town.[1]

To some this sudden death, so visibly visited from on high upon the head of a drunken old sinner, seemed a perfectly natural piece of divine judgment, a well-deserved punishment for insolence and insult; but to others it was almost a sign of special grace, seeing that providence had taken such apparent trouble on behalf of this poor mortal. Everyone, at any rate, was greatly dismayed and given pause for thought by this accident, so fraught with meaning. Only very late that night did the lights of the town die out.

The next day, with many curiosity-seekers

[1]Happily, the plan to preserve this unique house for posterity as the Powenz Museum has already been realized. It is open daily, except Mondays, from 9 A.M. to 6 P.M. Admission 50 pfennigs. Free on Sundays and holidays.

looking on, the vanished man's sons solemnly dug the black meteorite, as large as a man and still hot, up out of the earth. Their intent was to erect a monument worthy of their father on that very spot. Undoubtedly a peculiar symbol, this fizzled-out nocturnal rocket!

The stone's genuine meteoric origin, which had been publicly contested by malicious tongues, was confirmed as scientifically indisputable, to the great satisfaction of the bereaved who had requested the investigation. And inside the stone, where it was assayed with pumice and acid, there appeared enigmatic signs, ciphers and figures, like fragments of some secret code.

The old man's sons put a board fence up around this wonder of nature and charged people to see it. Violand Powenz, the deaf-mute, wrote a grisly little pamphlet about the stone; his brother Zephirin decorated it with pretty illustrations. It sold well.

When he was struck by the heavenly boulder, Baltus Powenz was seventy-seven years old. In all his long, eventful life he had never had a headache, and the sniffles only once, despite his having led a disorderly, even godless life, having drunk to excess and scandalizing many. In legitimate offspring alone, he left behind seven strong sons of diverse character and one especially beautiful daughter. Plus a wife who still looked like her own

In regard to this, see the above report
concerning Baltus Powenz's tragic end.

children's elder sister. And it was astonishing how greatly the poor woman grieved for him, even though, starting with their first night together, Powenz had beaten her with his painfully large hands almost daily his whole life long.

His sons and daughter Lilith also mourned him sincerely, if not overmuch. It may have comforted them that God, whose wrath against them and their father had never been all that earnest, had so neatly transformed the old codger back to nature and in the process had spared him the necessity for any funeral rites—something that he had always detested anyway.

The woods where the old man's song and laughter resounded, where he had made love and where of a sudden he would rush out and with a savage roar frighten peaceful citizens out for a walk—those woods devoured his few ashes and breathed in the blue smoke, making full use of him. No earthly trace of Powenz remained, not one small bone nor a tooth; nothing, that is, but a single strand of hair, taken from his four-year-old head, preserved by his mother and now handed on to posterity in all its blond innocence and with an angelic, silken luster somehow immortal.

Chapter Two

How and why Baltus Powenz came to
Moessel—His perseverance

M y first recollection of the departed is of his riding perilously through the streets of Moessel on a homemade high-wheel bicycle, to the amazement of many, since his was the first such vehicle. The tails of his old-fashioned brown formal coat were puffed full of wind like the wing case of a ladybug, lending him the appearance of some flying object, while for reasons of balance he held himself upright, stiff and haughty. In contrast to his formal coat he wore neither collar nor necktie, but only an ivory collar button.

At the time, he had opened a bike-riding school, the Velodrome, and for a while he had great fun watching the respectable Moesselers learning this newest of sports with great trials of terror and tumbles—all to the tune of a harp, on which instrument he was a master. He would sit in the middle of the track and shout in a booming voice: "Pedal! Pedal! Pedal!" while plucking away at "My Heart is Like a Beehive," a popular hit tune of the day. This went on until stout Herr Schurigl broke his neck, causing the sport to be placed under police supervision. Of course nothing ever happened to Powenz himself through all this. His sons, however, were born, one might say, with bicycles between their legs.

Baltus Powenz is said to have immigrated to Moessel during the early 1890's, but—so the report goes—quite by chance, almost by mistake. Actually, all he had wanted to do that day was to lay over till the next train, but there he had remained a full forty years, until the day of his abrupt and lamented demise.

Report has it further that not far from the railroad depot, in Adam's little brown wineshop, our passenger in transit, while quietly tippling, missed train after train. On that first evening he sat, it is said, in the same spot he would occupy almost every evening from that day until shortly before his death. He sat there all alone, smiling silently and affably into his wineglass. For three days, with the exception of a few hours that were slept away in the station waiting room, he drank, ever determined that with the next train he would most assuredly depart.

At first he was taken for a foreigner (if not, indeed, for a deaf-mute), for he would order all food and drink with only a finger pointed at the menu and a few encouraging nods. Or, if he wanted a refill, he tapped on his glass. He spoke not a word until the third day, when, along about midnight, he is said to have repeated one word, in German, several times over and with great fervor so that all could hear, ever and again just the one word: "Splendid, splendid!"

Tradition does not tell us, however, what the stranger meant that night by his exclamation, whether it was the wine, or the town perhaps, his life or the world at large, which he loved dearly. It is probable that in that very moment he came to his decision to settle for a time, or for good, in Moessel. That moment may thus be regarded as the real beginning of countless scandals and painful tribulations for the unsuspecting town of Moessel.

Baltus Powenz found things splendid in Adam's Wineshop, and he stayed.

There he sat, in those days beardless but with a head grown over with superabundant, very healthy and, as it were, hempen hair, much as if, like Samson's, it were charged with divine power. He sat there with gigantic hands and a broad, frank countenance that was graced with an almost never-failing animal goodwill—a face some might even call handsome—sat in silence for three days and drank, an enigmatic guest who evoked sympathy and curiosity as to who he was, what path had led him there and, finally, what his station in life might be.

He stayed, married, was fruitful and multiplied prodigiously.

All particulars about his origins, especially those he himself provided, are to be received with utmost caution. I find it impossible to decide if in truth he was, as rumor has it, a university dropout from a good family that had disowned him once and for all (some startling knowledge of medicine and jurisprudence, and of ancient languages as well, points in that direction); or if he was the son of a shepherd on the Luneburg Heath, which would explain his close harmony with nature; or if indeed he came from a family of hangmen, as was presumed in certain quarters.

For all the Powenzes were great and happy liars, both skilled and scrupulous in the art.

If at the time he had come, let us say, from Apolda or Pasewalk or Křimice, presumably fleeing some tiresome love affair, he would have had no trouble reporting that he had come directly from Paramaribo or Hyderabad. He rechristened that assuredly uncommonly common maid of Saxony, once named Emma or the like, and made of her a most charming Zaïde, then set his adventure in some teeming harbor city of India, in Pondicherry, for example, where he certainly had never been in all his life, while his ship, "the trim English steamer, the *Abukir*"—owing to a fatal case of plague on board—was forced to lie in quarantine

11

for weeks on end, in the most infernal heat, of course. And if someone in his audience really knew the place first hand, why then Powenz would depart posthaste on the next steamer of his imagination, but, as a result of a storm-swept crossing, from that point on he unfortunately had only the dimmest and vaguest of recollections. And all the time he blithely tossed around all sorts of nautical terminology, speaking of luff and lea, a capful of wind, of the davit and the mizzenmast, and chewed away on tobacco, skillfully spitting the golden brown juice in all directions.

There are photographs extant (soon on display to the general public in the Powenz Museum) that show Baltus Powenz sitting before a primitive tent, a tropical helmet on his head, a musket across his knees, with a freshly bagged gazelle lying next to him in the veldtgrass. Most of these exotic shots, produced with the aid of the unrivaled artistry of his dear son Zephirin, were taken in closest proximity to Moessel, out on the barren old Battle Moor[2] for instance, and the gazelle was a dead goat or just a throw rug.

It has been proven that Powenz gave public lectures in neighboring towns concerning his trips through Africa and Asia, illustrating them with Zephirin's lantern slides. The fraud was never dis-

[2] The scene of the Battle of Moessel, fought between the Swedes and the troops of the kaiser, August 3, 1633.

covered; on the contrary, both public and press expressed with the heartiest applause their thanks for his thrilling commentary.

Powenz was of the opinion that the only legitimate lies were the ones that stayed undiscovered. For him the only sinful thing about lying was the disappointment and ignominy of having been lied to. The true lie, however, must remain the secret of its originator. And for that reason Powenz met all skeptics with the most glorious intransigence. He was prepared at any time to stake his very life on the veracity of his lies.

And so it happened that in all seriousness he once let things come to a duel because a chance guest in Adam's Wineshop began, on the perfectly justifiable basis of personal experience, to cast doubt upon Powenz's sober report of his adventures among the walruses of the Arctic and upon the veracity of the bloodthirsty tale entitled "My First Bengal Tiger."

In the course of this duel (the Court of Honor having changed the challenge with pistols to combat with heavy sabers), this colossal teller of tales made a most woeful mess of that truth-loving meddler. By thus vindicating his honor, Powenz had made his reputation for years to come.

The scene of the duel was an idyllic forest glade, to which many years later the brave father led his numerous adolescent sons and most vividly demonstrated the entire proceedings to them. To mark the spot, his gallant sons erected a memorial tablet still well worth seeing. On it, the mighty Powenz is pictured lunging forward to deliver a quarte to the face of his opponent, whose fencing abilities were pretty wretched. The referee wears a top hat; bespectacled doctors are already busy in the foreground with bandages and instruments, while in the background a black four-wheeled coach stands waiting. This picture, too, was the work of the ingenious Zephirin. It was painted on durable copper, and from a distance the whole thing resembles a roadside religious shrine.

Immediately after his arrival in Moessel, Powenz seems to have declared openly and cheerfully to everyone his intent to settle permanently, by which he meant either purchasing a house or building one, although he had no money at all, a fact that seemed not to depress him in the least. He had arrived without baggage, dressed in a check inverness, the very same one that he was wearing when the star dispatched him; and most likely he lived miserably enough for some time, defraying his living expenses in various ways, since it struck him as far too boring to pursue the same profession one's whole life long.

Certainly, he was able to do no end of things —all of them quite charming, to be sure, but none of them of any fundamental use whatever. He

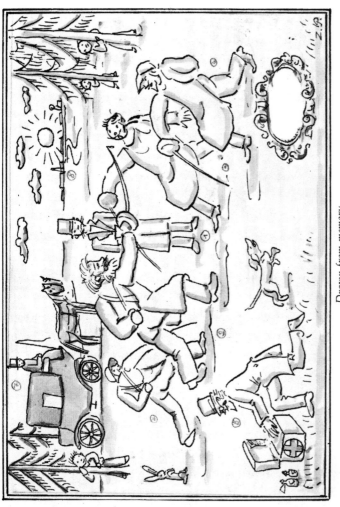

Drawn from memory
(1) The referee (2) Father (3) His opponent
(4) The seconds (5) Dr. Flaum (7) Coach
(8) Town of Moessel

was, for example, a master at constructing the paper kites that every autumn filled the heavens above Moessel as if with ranks of angels. He lived, one might say, on air. Golden Christmas angels with pleated skirts were among his specialties, too. His strong point, however, was the invention and manufacture of all sorts of novelty items, invented for the amusement and vexation of his fellow man; chief among these were fireworks, itching powder and sneezing powder ("Blow a pinch into the parlor and everyone there will sneeze—dandy good fun.") But there were sundry other highly original items for teasing, twitting and tricking guileless souls; for instance, that old favorite, the Din Disc ("Toss it on the floor when no one is looking and it sets up an ear-splitting racket—particularly good for annoying the lady of the house.") Other specialties included his superb exploding cigars and so-called stink bombs.

He also employed his genius in the invention of a device for securing bicycles against theft. He very cleverly mounted a needle under the cleft in the seat so that it popped up whenever an unauthorized person swung up onto the bike. Powenz unfortunately forgot one time to disconnect the insidious apparatus and got a most painful taste of the incontestable advantages of his invention.[3]

[3]Patent pending.

Age 1   Age 10

Age 17   Age 26

Baltus Powenz
at four different stages of life

Chapter Three

Concerns the first automobile in Moessel,
a beach and a walking picture-book

Although he was possibly Moessel's chief pauper, it was Powenz's ambition to be the first person to own a real automobile—not a brand-new factory model, of course, but a do-it-yourself version.

With Job-like patience and exemplary hard work, he succeeded in building at least a sort of automobile out of diverse junk parts from ancient vehicles and machines. It was not lovely to look at, with nothing at all elegant or sporty about its lines, but he lacquered it a bright red and yellow, and it most resembled one of those merry-go-round carts that very small children ride in when they are not yet big enough for the horses. The Powenz Motorcar appeared to be of greater antiquity than any horse-drawn coach of the day; it made an atrocious noise and gave off an unbearable stench. One got the impression it lived on continual explosions that it then spewed out puffing and reeking from its underbelly like incessant sneezes. It could, moreover, only be driven either very fast or at a snail's pace. Horses and cows shied at its approach as if it were some hellish deity.

Nevertheless, people were jealous of his fame as an apostle of progress. Steps were taken officially to forbid him the use of this nuisance. But then one day the district doctor's horse dropped dead out on the road, and it was Powenz's good luck to be able to give a lift to the doctor, who arrived just in time to assist at a difficult delivery—and so Powenz helped save two human lives. They let him keep his car. Shortly thereafter, he pawned the legendary vehicle. It stood in a wagon shed for many years, unsold and unsellable, but so well preserved that later it could be purchased for the Powenz Museum, where it is a special jewel in the collection.

During the summers, however, he ran a small silver-gray private beach. It was situated not far from town on charming Powenz Island, which was named for him very early on. It was a lazy kind of job that suited him just fine; the lease was cheap, and he could run around more or less naked all summer in just his red and white striped bathing suit and an immense straw hat, doing nothing and living very inexpensively all the while.

He led the life of an Indian, eating fish that he would catch himself and roast on a stick, and salads of mixed greens provided by Mother Nature, chiefly sorrel and cresses. He slept on a coconut mat in one of the very simple changing cabins.

It is said that even then he had begun to collect building materials, and not always of the unclaimed sort, with a view to the house that he one day intended to own, come what might. He could often be seen wandering among the meadows, a roofing tile or perhaps some useable board clasped under his arm like a loaf of bread, his face beaming with delight. He is also the source of the exclamation one frequently hears when someone spots a store-yard of building materials: "Ah, what beautiful bricks!"

In those days, however, he was still very well liked, and his body, which bore fabulous tattooings, brought a smile to people's lips. When in summer, nicely suntanned, he would stride along his beach, he became a walking picture book, offering entertainment to the younger folk, who never wearied of gazing at the rich variety of this work of art. A fat, diamondback snake, for example, wound its way up his right leg; on his chest Paradise could be seen, with Adam, Eve and all the beasts—giraffes, elephants, lions, crocodiles and bats. His broad back was adorned with a group portrait of the kaiser and family beneath which was inscribed "Learn to suffer in silence." Underneath that were the earth's two hemispheres surrounded by sun, moon and stars. Along his ribs on both sides were engraved, as if on some calendar chart, the principal dates of his life. Two squirrels,

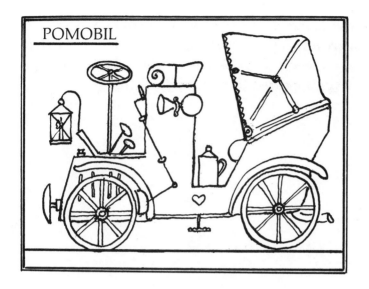

POMOBIL

one after the other, chased around his left leg as if they were playing tag on the trunk of a tree. His right arm was engraved with a wristwatch that always gave the time as half-past five. He would sometimes push up his sleeve with inimitable grandeur and look at this ersatz watch. The Powenzes never owned a real clock. "The man who has no clock always has the time" (Baltus Powenz, *Maxims*). In addition to the watch, there were pistols and a hand raised in solemn oath; on his left arm was an angel plucking a harp.

But on the pectoral muscle above his heart, apparently, was his dream house, drawn a bit clumsily, much as a child might draw it in ink, with a smoking chimney, trees to the right and left and a great many windows, all somewhat out of kilter.

Owing to these illustrations, Baltus Powenz never appeared to be totally naked.

Chapter Four

*Tells of wedded love, of fertility
and of justice*

An event of some savagery occurred at this period. As Powenz was making love to a girl in the woods one summer day, he was disturbed in the midst of his merry dalliance by two insufferably curious lads; furious and clad only in his bluish pictures, the man is said to have sprung up out of the bushes like a faun, grabbed them both roughly by their angelic curls and then banged the heads of the meddlesome intruders together hard a few times, in order to teach them "more respect for love." *Relata refero!*

The mighty hahaha of Powenz's laughter echoed down through that lovely German wood in pursuit of the two chastized boys.

For good reason this incident stirred up general indignation in Moessel, an indignation that was subsequently to grow still greater. For Powenz now rented a small garret in a cheerless, sooty house near the railroad tracks and married an uncommonly affectionate maiden from the village of Kyps. She already had had one son by him, the almost three-year-old Kaspar, and her tender frame was now big with yet another child.

The wedding, therefore, was a strictly private affair. Little Kaspar strewed flowers, Powenz got drunk and struck his wife, while she was moved to loud blubberings. When Powenz was intoxicated, his behavior could be quite appalling, and so it happened that in the frenzy of that night he slung their new featherbeds and pillows—practically the whole of his wife's dowry—over his head and shoulders and lugged the swaying burden up onto the roof, where, once he had slit open the ticking, he sat straddling the ridge and let the feathers snow down out of the balmy summer night sky in a dazzling improvisation of winter, all the while singing in a lugubrious voice an old song about a hunchbacked dwarf.

The uproar may have contributed to the young woman's going into labor in the wee hours of her wedding night, bearing a second son whom his father named Fabian (which means "he who cultivates the bean").

In the space of ten years she was to bring a rough total of seven live children into this world, among them one daughter. The third, however, was a son, the rather melancholy Heinrich. Powenz himself assisted at the birth with his own hands, sans midwife or physician.

In fact Powenz did most everything himself

from the start—truth to tell, he had to. The few articles his wife had contributed to their household were soon pawned when hard times came and were never redeemed. Replacements were necessary if the hard-pressed family did not want to go on camping amid bare rooms in picturesque poverty.

It seems incomprehensible, and I am afraid that the Moesselers never did quite comprehend it, that a man in such strappingly good health and with such a lust for life, with his unusual practical talent for things like cabinetmaking, tinsmithy, medicine, electronics, pettifoggery and so on— that such a man did not simply cultivate one of his hundred occupations and practice it as an upstanding member of the local citizenry. But that is not what Powenz wanted. The long and short of it was that he had a most unorthodox kind of love of personal freedom.

We know that in all his many small legal battles he acted as his own lawyer. For instance, in the memorable suit that his neighbor Herr Gockeley, who disliked him intensely, brought against him for illegally using the title of Doctor, Gockeley came armed with two well-known legal advisors while Powenz appeared with only a large blue portfolio, very much like a schoolboy's notebook— and he carried the day.

There is documented evidence that Herr Adam,

the owner of the small brown wineshop, is at fault for Powenz's having never been called anything but Doctor Powenz in Moessel from almost the very beginning. Perhaps Adam conferred the title on him because the stranger had casually spoken of "occupying a chair." And even if, as Powenz contended, he had modestly and unequivocally demurred, "No titles, please, none!" the *Doctor* stuck with him; through no fault of his own and quite improperly, it stuck with him despite its being later repeatedly contested by his opponents and their having secured a restraining order forbidding him, under penalty of law, from using said title.

Indeed, out of pure inadvertent thoughtlessness (and how annoying it must have been after it was all over), the presiding judge in the case addressed the accused with precisely the title that was being legally challenged, that is, as *Doctor* Powenz. With cunning indignation, however, Powenz at once forbade any such usage, and so demonstratively and impressively documented his innocence in public. To all appearances deeply wounded, he spoke of being openly ridiculed and, to the surprise of those present, cited by heart the legal paragraphs that protect the accused from open humiliation before the bar.

The Powenz boys enthusiastically applauded their father and with wide grins still on their faces, they were removed from the courtroom.

After the gentle Heinrich, Lilith entered this world, a girl with great brown eyes swimming in what was at first a bluish white and clammy face that did not look quite done yet, since she had been born prematurely. She was an unusually ugly and loathesome child, quite early disposed to biting, spitting and screeching—a little devil even then.

The next son was called Violand, a name that Powenz himself invented. The circumstances of his birth were peculiar. Powenz had been in the best of moods, joking with his wife all that evening; she finally had to laugh so wholeheartedly that the jovial joltings brought on her labor pains.

Since, sad to say, Powenz had fallen out with the church, he did not have Violand and the children that followed him baptized—neither Violand, that versatile child with such a lovely, eloquent voice (his father's favorite, one might add), nor the merry, artistic Zephirin. For a long time the youngest child was a lad with the equally heathenish name of Jadup; though actually one of a set of twins, he had suffocated his more delicate sister in the cradle before three days had gone by—a quite innocent accident, but one heavy with symbolic meaning in view of the lack of charity he would later display toward his fellow man. He was a creature filled with a serene cruelty—and yet, he was inordinately attractive.

Frau Powenz, however, worried greatly about the poor souls of her little ones and baptized them herself in secret, employing a rite she had invented, which consisted of dropping a little wine, mixed with dust, onto the innocent heads and of brushing their tiny mouths with a flower.

As might be expected, Powenzian fertility was a cause for public scandal in the town of Moessel.[4] The town was embodied above all in the per-

[4]At this point I shall allow myself a brief note concerning the town's geography, etc.: Moessel, from the Latin *Castellum moselinum*, OHG mûzzelaha, is situated on the Maar River, noted for its excellent fishing (pop. 14,692; 975 ft. above sea level), and in times past was immediately subject to the kaiser. Today it is a peaceful country town set in pleasant surroundings. A half day suffices for a visit. Hotels and inns: "The Whale" (Napoleon slept here in 1806), with shaded garden and rooms at 1 mark and up. "The Golden Glove," good home cooking, recommended. "The Mole" (clean), "The Red Cow" (simple). Wine can be had at Adam's near the train station. History: According to legend, Moessel was founded by Charles the Fat (see above). Completely razed by the Huns in 955, it recovered only very slowly. After a short blossoming in the middle ages, especially under the cultured Count Kasimir XIII, the major portion of the town was destroyed by a disastrous fire during the Thirty Years' War. From 1700 to 1783, it was the residence of the Dowager Duchess Anna. Moessel owes its present prosperity to the industry and hard work of its citizens. Principal manufactures are toys, bobbin lace and picture postcards, plus viticulture. Tour: Beginning at the train station (simple red brick) and walking past the post office, one comes directly to the former ducal country residence (now a pawnshop). Before it the lovely marble monument (by Bernauer) to the unfortunate Queen Luise. To the left, the Town Hall built by Knipfel in neo-gothic style, 1899–1901. Behind it, the city park with fine old trees. Fountains. Worth a visit is the protestant church of St. Moritz with its ancient gravestones. In good weather, a rewarding panorama from the steeple; the key can be had from the sextant across the way (a small gratuity is sug-

son of one Frau Quiebus. This gigantic lady, of whom we shall frequently need speak, was the archenemy of the Powenz pack; she expressed to everyone her candid opinion that there ought to be a stop to such shocking, indeed shameful, goings-on—with the help of the police, if need be.

gested). From there to the primary school and market place. House No. 7 (at street level, a stocking shop) bears a bronze plaque honoring the local poet, Karl Butter (1802–1873), born here, though now quite unjustly forgotten. Excursions: over the vineyard hill (red markers) in the direction of Schneppers (three-quarters of an hour, lovely view from the inn). We recommend a walk along the Maar River to the idyllic Powder Woods (gnat-infested in summer). Here, an island with a beach for swimming. Canoe rental.

Chapter Five

Behold, how beautiful it is when brothers
live together in peace.

The Powenz apartment was small and consisted exclusively of sleeping quarters. Bunk beds were soon a necessity. The children's clothes, sewn by their mother, were handed down from Kaspar even unto Jadup. Boots and stockings were to be had only in winter, since in summer all Powenzes ran around barefoot, wearing only a shirt and short pants, and tanned golden brown— except for countless white scars, for one of them was almost always wounded. Although they washed but probably hardly ever brushed their teeth, the impression they gave, as I remember it, was one of natural cleanliness. Their hair grew wild as if made of string or sauerkraut. To save on barber bills, Powenz trimmed it himself by clapping a pot of appropriate size down onto each boy's head and simply lopping off what stuck out from under it.

In summer, so it seemed, they lived almost exclusively on blueberries—laughing with blue teeth for all the world to see.

During their early childhood years, the Powenzes were never known to have played ring-around-the-rosy or even bunny-in-the-hole. In their loose-fitting clothes, and especially in the kind of shorts with straps that button at the shoulders, they would roll around all day in the gutter; like plants, they took in nourishment from the earth through their skin—from the earth, sand and mud, for they had an ineffable love of water. Water, fire, air and earth were their favorite toys.

The story is told that Jadup, ever thirsty for knowledge, ate dirt, that in fact there was nothing he did not try to eat. He had to have at least one taste of everything that came from nature.

Concerning these grimy Powenz rascals, Frau Quiebus once said, "They are animals." But they were the most sought after pinboys in Moessel and were unrivaled as ball boys out on the tennis courts. They were fully proficient at kite-flying, stilt-walking and marble-shooting. They were unsurpassed masters at playing wild Indians. Apparently using his father as prototype, Zephirin would paint their naked bodies. He did his best work on sleepy Fabian, who stood still the longest.

But it was held against them that without much ado they would likewise strip innocent little girls of their clothing—Frau Quiebus's daughter, for instance—and paint them from head to toe with all sorts of beasts and totems.

Sad to say, these cheeky lads were also caught going about unabashedly begging. They knew how to strike gruesome poses and to imitate the most pitiful of cripples. Jadup in particular used this method for earning his cigarette money. And the Powenz boys all started smoking at the tender age of six. At first, of course, they rolled their own, using beech leaves that stank dreadfully and made them slightly sick.

They were indeed a frightful pack, always pummeling one another, but facing the outside world with a united front—robber barons, bellicose and feared. One of their favorite words was "ripping."

I would often see them returning home from battle, hot and hungry, breathing through moist, open mouths and distended nostrils, their brown necks bloodied or dusted a satiny white. They always carried acacia switches, a favorite thorny weapon for cutting and thrusting, or slingshots made from a forked tree branch, preferably from hazelwood, which is both firm and pliant. A piece of leather—a glove remnant worked best—was fastened at both ends with shoelaces, and then, of course, firm but resiliant rubber tubing was inserted between prongs and leather. Small fowl (sparrows, blackbirds, doves) were easily felled with this weapon. Kaspar, the eldest, maintained he had once used it to shoot a rabbit that had been harried and huzzahed into a stone quarry and, unable to escape, had thrown itself in desperation against the steep red sandstone walls.

When teased, as he often was, by his brothers because of his illegitimate birth, Kaspar would become very angry. He kept rugged but effective discipline among his younger brothers, for he was strong and merciless. He would simply grab the smaller ones by the waistband and hang them on a hook from the ceiling of the room, often letting them dangle there for hours on end.

At age sixteen he was already the father of a baby boy (and the elder Powenz exerted himself mightily both in giving his irresponsible son an earnest talking-to and in extricating himself and Kaspar from all financial obligations). Thus very early on, he had earned a reputation as the boldest lover in town.

The Powenz pack did not reside somewhere, they bivouacked. They all grew up wild, one might say, in a town filled for the most part with peaceable widows of clergymen and with honest pensioners.

An extra large crate, on which was stenciled black lettering that read, "Express: Caution! This End Up!" served as the family table, with smaller crates for chairs. The large crate was fitted with a trapdoor so that whichever child was the most mutinous at the moment could be caged inside it; the child, however, could take revenge by pinching and tickling the legs of the others seated around the table. Parts of the bunk beds came from old ladders, making them look something like hayracks in a barn. Banners of wash crisscrossed the rooms in a permanent draping of flags, and clothes dangled like hanged men from hooks in the ceiling, there being neither closet nor wardrobe.

One consequence of these domestic herdings was that the Powenz children all had the whooping cough more or less at once, and their desperate fits of coughing, known to aggravate the spasms associated with the disease, sounded truly alarming, especially at night. They would sit in their bunk beds, their faces almost blue with croaking, yelping and whooping; finally Powenz simply forbade them to cough, with any infraction to be punished by a barbaric flogging—which threat he proceeded to carry out. This Russian whipping cure for whooping cough proved quite effective. It helped little Jadup not in the least when he whined, "I'm not coughing, it's coughing all on its own!" Whoever coughed got a lashing—ergo they coughed no more. But in order that they might be recognized at a distance as an infectious danger to the public at large and so be avoided, around their necks were strung tags that read, "I have the whooping cough!"[5] When they gargled they made coloratura music together.

Nails or splinters in the foot were allowed to fester their way back out; bleeding was stopped with compresses of snuff.

[5]A great consolation for the young mothers of the town!

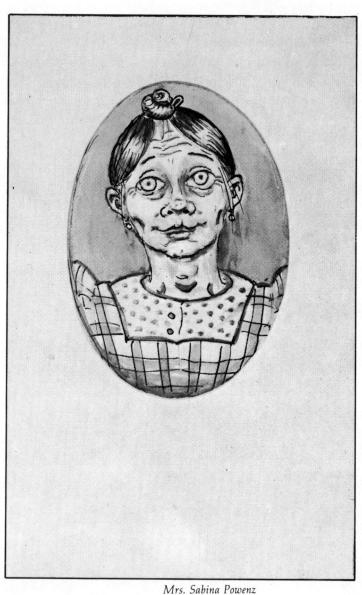

Mrs. Sabina Powenz

Chapter Six

Deals briefly with the diet and daily needs
of the Powenz pack

All the time his lads were growing up in this fashion, Powenz himself never lost sight of his one great goal: the house.

When he would walk along the street or across open country, he could be seen suddenly to bend over and pick something up, examining and testing it.

Powenz collected things.

Wherever he was, he looked for building materials for his dream house, and he always found something, if only a nail or a screw, while the finding of a brick was a glorious occasion. Whatever was of some use he slipped into his pocket and then stowed under the beds at home. By his calculations, if all his boys were to collect as he did, he would soon have enough basics to build his house.

But in the meantime, the way Powenz and his family chose to live simply would not do. It really was quite improper; it simply had to create scandal; it was an outrage for a respectable town.

The children always addressed their mother (just as they did their father) familiarly by her forename, Sabina; whereas she called her husband Herr Powenz. It was doubtless with the best intentions that she used particularly conspicuous patches for the repair of the countless holes, tears and gaps in the clothing that was handed down from Kaspar to Jadup on its way toward dissolution. She would use swatches of red checks or blue polka dots, whatever was colorful and bright, until in their pied raggedness, they all resembled impoverished harlequins in three-quarter-length pants. Often there was absolutely nothing left of the original material the clothing was made of. It renewed itself the way human skin does.

When holes wore through winter stockings, the skin underneath was blackened with a bit of ink.

There was a persistent, though not unchallenged, rumor—intended presumably to arouse disgust—that the Powenz pack lived chiefly on crow meat; and it was assumed as a matter of course that they dined on mice, frogs, snakes and worms the way other people eat oysters, crab and caviar. That from time to time they did eat roast cat has been established with some certainty.

Chapter Seven

Why, with even the best of intentions,
one could still run afoul of the Powenz pack

It was really no one's business, to be sure,
but...

The lovely little garden neighboring on the
Powenzes' belonged to the distinguished councilman Herr Gockeley (whose grudge against the
family was not unfounded). How had it happened
that instead of the vegetables and flowers he had
planted, there had sprouted nettles, dandelions,
thistles and other weeds, all in such prettily
ordered rows that at first Gockeley did not even
notice what was blooming there! It appeared as if
the point was to prove just how beautiful these
despised plants could look when planted row on
row, how much they seemed to like it there, how
they throve in the fertile black beds of this rich
neighbor! And most certainly it was the tattered
and patched Powenz pack that had done this to
him. Everyone knew it, but no one could prove it.

What must have been the painstaking labor
necessary for such a mean trick to succeed? How
constant must the hate have been and what

patience must it have taken to gather seeds a whole year long and store them in carefully labeled packets? The deed itself had cost a night's sleep and required the most delicate precautionary measures for everything to appear perfectly normal. The boys were aided by an admirable knowledge of botany; this enabled them to substitute the weeds while the plants were still germinating or just sprouting. The enemy noticed only after it was too late.

And who, I ask, were the desperados strongly suspected of having broken into Fromm's Boarding School for Girls and dumping effervescent salts into the chamber pots, which, as might be expected, caused great terror among the poor girls?

Who had sent every last old maid in Moessel (and there were close to 200 of them) a tender note perfumed with May flowers and requesting a rendezvous—all on the same day, at the same time and in the same place? And who then took secret photographs of the assemblage?

Who is to be held responsible for the many convincing hauntings that occurred in all parts of the superstitious town?

And finally, who thought up all the slanderous nicknames, the merciless characterizations that honest folks quietly had to admit were quite apt; by which, for example, the good but somewhat bug-eyed pastor was universally called God's Frog? Oh, the Powenzian tricks were many.

Despite all of this, several Powenzes managed to attend Moessel Academic High with some success, for longer or shorter periods of time. Kaspar, Fabian, Violand and Jadup were a scourge to their pitiable teachers, but were equally loved and feared by their schoolmates. They were masters at copying from others and carried on a lucrative trade in ponies and cribs ("Prepared by a Scholar") and handy miniature lexica in flesh-colored bindings. In all such matters, they owed their dear father a great deal, for when Powenz was in a good mood, he would tell his sons all sorts of intimate tales from his own youth. And how gladly did the boys listen! From him they learned how to behave in school; he showed them the ins and outs, the priceless stratagems thanks to which they were able to meet class standards with a minimum of time and effort. He taught them to deal with their fellow men—as, for example, with the strict school principal—with a blithe fearlessness: one had only to imagine them stark naked or in the midst of the act of love. He also gave them his own time-tested tips on how to handle girls.

They had, sad to say, little respect for the dignity of man.

Chapter Eight

Devoted to the varied talents of the family

Mention has already been made of "Doctor" Powenz's masterful plucking on the harp. He owned a beautiful instrument, gilded and ornamented with the charming head of a cherub.

He never once pawned this harp—he would rather have starved.

His sons, too, were musicians. Kaspar could blow expressively on the trombone; Fabian, the most musical but also the laziest, handled the tympani; Heinrich listened. The cello was played by their wild sister and the flute by Zephirin. Violand was content to play the harmonica and was, in fact, a virtuoso on it. Finally, Jadup sang with a pure angelic voice even as a small boy, and he could also fiddle quite prettily.

When this unusual Powenz band assembled to play music, the neighbors would shudder and the house would shake. Because of the family's cramped living quarters, the instruments hung from the ceiling and were let down at the start of a concert and raised again at its conclusion. Their concerts were quite properly cursed as music from hell, as a vile sacrilege of the arts—particularly since they had the effrontery to adapt even Bach, Mozart and Beethoven for their orchestra. Fabian was particularly daring in his arrangements. They were all charged with malicious mischief and with disturbing the town's nocturnal peace.

It is reported that wicked Powenz, seated at his harp and directing with both gigantic hands, never wept except when playing especially beautiful music—Schubert's Trio in B Major, for example.

Powenz indulged himself in many and varied occupations. This can be inferred from a collection of homemade signs, all of which at one time or other were affixed to his door and were frequently changed. They have fortunately been preserved almost in their entirety. Among them, to name just a few of the many, are: "Modern Technical Specialities," then "Powenz School of Music, from Beginners to Masters" (this from a period in which he gave harp lessons), plus "Uncle Baltus's Doll Hospital," "Universal Bicycle School," and in bold letters "Manufacturer of Novelties and Fancy Goods: The Oldest Firm on the Square," and much more of the same.

Later on, when Powenz's bad boys were old enough to be of some real service, a business of a sort did develop out of these very modest beginnings. Doctor Powenz called this subdivision of his talents "Pyrotechnical Laboratories," and it was there that as the inventive and talented German toy maker he truly was, he constructed brilliant pinwheels, fiery serpents, starry pyramids, single and double comets—everything, in fact, that makes for a merry display of fireworks. Powenz, then, created nothing lasting, but without question he created things that were beautiful and free, things that soared heavenwards only to explode and expire in pure delight.

Yes indeed, Powenz seemed to have been sent by the devil himself, for he understood how to play with fire so splendidly, and he loved fire so much, that a bit of the stench always clung to him when it was all over.

Taught very early to live on their own wits and resources, the Powenz boys loved best to live off other people's parties and festivities. They were all equally adept at walking on their hands as at walking on their feet.

It was always a pleasure at some summer gala in Moessel to hear little Jadup lift his voice to sing an enchantingly gruesome ballad, fully illustrated with grisly pictures painted by Zephirin's own hand.

Lilith, saucy and yet ever so aloof, took up the collection while she read palms on the side, sometimes telling gentlemen some very intimate fortunes.

Violand, always a deceiver, could do magic
tricks, and Kaspar the Strong Man's act included
one of those ever-popular gigantic thermometer-
like apparatuses used to test muscle power.

Frau Powenz, of course, had her hands full
with her "seven plagues," and I never saw her fold
them idly in her lap. She was always on the go,
darning, mending, washing for her boys—yet she
never got any older. She would mend three-
cornered tears on the spot, laying the child alive
and kicking across her lap and sometimes sewing
some skin along with the fabric.

The whole town knew that it was Powenz's
custom to give each of his children a sound thrashing every morning—in advance, so that it could be
worked off during the day.

Powenz himself admitted good-naturedly that
at that hour he had them all so nicely together and
that, besides, they were still half-asleep and so
could put up little resistance with their drowsy,
feeble hands. There were certainly some awful
scenes sometimes, and Frau Powenz, caught quite
innocently in the thick of battle, would raise her
arms and wail loudly. Lilith had the right to hand
Powenz his malacca cane—that is if the boys had
not smoked it, something they had been known to
do. It made them, they confessed, so wonderfully
sick. And should their father forget the thrashing,
which seldom happened, the boys would remind

him of it. Otherwise something that made for a good and healthy life would have been missing.

Despite everything, Powenz always proved master of his boys' allied forces, although they stoutheartedly attacked the old bruiser from all sides with scratches, kicks and tugs at his beard or with long-range missiles of books, slippers, pots and potatoes. And it really was wonderful to watch this splendid man do battle with his own flesh and blood, with the fruit of his loins, always triumphing in the end and saying that that would teach them to raise a hand against their own father.

It often happened, however, that in the midst of these bloody scuffles one of the combatants—the nimble Violand, perhaps, or the lithe Jadup, the mighty Kaspar or the father himself—would execute some especially good defensive move, invent a new hold or a new subterfuge, or manage some brilliant feat of gymnastics; and then the others would all stop in admiration, clapping and offering loud praise, only too glad to have a demonstration of the stroke so that they, too, might learn it. They were proud when their father patted them on the shoulder in recognition or, as sometimes happened, even gave them a kiss. And then their careworn mother would smile amidst her tears, though insisting that she was not laughing but crying!

Once Powenz struck his wife, and Frau Quiebus, who had just happened to drop in, interposed. Frau Powenz, however, planted both arms on her hips and in true Powenz fashion spoke the classic words: "What business is it of yours if my dear husband hits me!" Frau Quiebus retreated in confusion.

The reader may wonder how under such circumstances anyone could tolerate troublesome tenants like these in his house. And in fact there were years in which the Powenz family was unfortunately obliged to change its place of residence three or even seven times.

This was always the occasion for a high and solemn procession through the whole town. At its head was darling Jadup, outfitted with goose wings in the role of Cupid the god of love (just as he was also very useful as a *postillon d'amour*, or messenger of love, for his brothers). He blew merry tunes on a harmonica. Behind him came Zephirin bearing the Powenz family banner (a white house on a red background); then, as a kind of honorary virgin, Lilith strewing flowers. Next came the four oldest boys, who bore a bed by its four legs like a baldachin above their heads, beneath which King Baltus could be seen, on his head a paper crown, in his hands a brick that served as his orb and a bottle of red wine for a scepter, from which he took a good pull every now and then. Bringing up the rear marched Frau

Powenz, a kerosene lamp in hand. Gentle Heinrich's little menagerie always caused quite a stir; it consisted of a hedgehog, two squirrels, countless guinea pigs, turtles, snakes, newts and an awfully clever raven named Wugg, whom the good-for-nothing children had with infinite patience taught nasty and indecent expressions such as: "Oh, you dingbat!" or "Beat it, stupid!" The bird blinked archly when it spoke and stuck out the tip of its tongue, just the way Heinrich did.

The most difficult task each time, of course, was the transporting of the building materials for Powenz's dream house, particularly those magnificent bricks. They were all carefully numbered, and the total grew slowly but steadily. Powenz could always give you the exact tally at any given time. They were tossed in relay like dumbbells from one end of town to the other—the same method used for other, smaller objects such as boots and dishes—all executed with a dancelike grace. Whenever the family moved, Powenz would bear with an air of mystery several rolls of paper—the detailed plans for the house.

Widow Quiebus
from a contemporary portrait

Chapter Nine

*The obstinancy and very dubious manners
of the Powenzes—Their natural enemies*

The Powenz family contributed little to the general public welfare, and its enemies were many. When one considers that almost two-thirds of the town's population consisted of retirees and widows of clergymen plus their daughters, then one understands the resistance with which they necessarily met the free opinions, lax morals and above all the outrageous sensuality of the Powenz family. Could one allow a respectable girl to walk across the street (not to mention across a country meadow) with an easy heart, as long as these wild and hairy fiends, these "lascivious ruffians" were running around loose? Was it not disgusting the way Powenz himself publicly boasted of being a love child? It was all an abomination for Moessel of the Hundred Eyes—a name Powenz once bestowed upon the town with such fine irony in one of his speeches; it is probably an allusion to those door gadgets, very common in Moessel, popularly called peepholes. Had not even immoral Frau von S—— had to eat humble pie as the result of a rare unanimity among all Moesselers in her case? (She had had the impudence to wear in public a bracelet with a charm made from the bullet with which her cuckolded husband had shot her lover.) Why then should the Powenzes not be treated likewise?

At that time there were approximately 7,000 widows and dependent daughters in Moessel. They all dressed in black, which did not lend the town a very lively appearance. Over them all, however, ruled the rich widow Quiebus, a pink and very corpulent giant of a lady. She loved to do works of charity, but she hated the Powenz pack. She abhorred them, perhaps because her well-meaning attempt to save these terribly neglected children had misfired on three occasions; and it is old and common knowledge that one can raise other people's children better than one can one's own. But nothing could in truth have offended the obstinate Powenzes more than for someone to want to lead them back onto the path of righteousness.

It may also be that Frau Quiebus guessed who it was that for a considerable length of time anonymously sent her small free samples of a remedy for obesity and gigantism by every morning's post. It may also be that she saw a reference to herself in the numerous caricatures—some of them in color —that Zephirin's impudent hand had drawn on highly visible walls all over town. They portrayed a fat lady, insultingly mustachioed, who was forced to roll around her monstrous belly in front of her in a wagon, while buildings collapsed all about her from the tremors set off by her steps. Or a depiction (and this horrid picture was painted on the main post office) of the same lady who had affixed a cluster of brightly colored balloons to her corpulent body in order to facilitate forward motion. Or another that pictured a lad, who resembled little Jadup, walking in front of her and carrying the burden of her belly in a rucksack. To the great amusement of the townspeople, these paintings appeared in ever new variations (one showed a donkey as the porter) and were attributed to the Powenz pack, who, of course, stubbornly denied having anything to do with their creation.

Nevertheless, the deeply offended lady never forgot who the malefactors were. She became their bitterest enemy, and from then on she managed to pin responsibility automatically on the Powenzes for every crime committed in Moessel. She considered the scoundrels capable of every sort of theft or arson, even murder.

Though one may have a great urge to annoy one's fellow man, that does not necessarily mean that one must also hate him or her. The Powenzes set about with the greatest enthusiasm to annoy

Frau Quiebus, but when all was said and done, they actually liked her.

Frau Thusnelda Quiebus had the figure of a statue of Germania. She was blond, red-cheeked and, as mentioned before, colossal. She was that way because she ate too much, although of course she flatly denied it. Almost all fat people maintain that they eat almost nothing and do not know why they are constantly putting on weight. Frau Quiebus said the same of herself. That little bit of soup, those few potatoes, that little sliver of cake and whipped cream—why, they couldn't possibly be the reason. It simply had to be some predisposition of the body (glands, perhaps?) that caused it—or maybe her seamstress, whose clothes always made her look so terribly fat. In terms of her figure, Frau Quiebus could without doubt have served as the town goddess (in the ancient sense of the word). For symbolic effect, let us imagine this unforgettable lady completely covered, like her great adversary Baltus Powenz, with tattoos, but with hers depicting a plan of the town of Moessel, a bird's-eye view, so to speak, with church, post office and train station; our symbol is meant to demonstrate that everything that happened in town happened to her, moved her both physically and emotionally. Her soul was in labor with every child born in town; she wept and died at each death; and above all, she took warm part in every love affair. She countenanced no secrets anywhere in town, and the town shook beneath her martial footfall. "Kunibert," she is supposed to have once said to her late husband, "I am the town!"

Ah, poor Anna Fehling, you, for example—if you want to keep your love a secret, then arm your heart with plates of steel as thick as a man's fist. No one knows yet that you are in love, my pale maid from a respectable family; you yourself are hardly aware of it yet. But Frau Quiebus has long since surmised it. Oh Anna, be careful, lest you meet her just at that moment when your love-filled eyes will betray you. The smallest glance and you are found out. Frau Quiebus knows that tell-tale glint of the eyes; you cannot pretend with her, my young miss. And why? Why because she has been in love herself. She does not really know why it is that all the young girls in Moessel come to her quite on their own to pour out their hearts to her. But they pour out their hearts, and Frau Quiebus touches and sniffs at them, turns each heart inside out as if it were her purse, leaving nothing inside, though sometimes the contents do get a bit mixed-up when placed in those gigantic pink hands of hers.

"Child," Frau Quiebus says finally, kissing the bewildered girl, "my only advice is, don't get tied down too early in life."

Frau Quiebus has a sympathetic heart. She weeps with everyone in his or her affliction, with the mailman, with the cleaning lady, even with the tax agent. She has a great human understanding for all things. Oh, she understands Frau Uhlenkamp's weakness, has long known about it; nor does she condemn pretty Frau Jorkum. She knows the delicate origin of Herr Director L——'s spinal-cord complaint and knows for certain why the O——'s are childless. She is well-informed about everything, has precise information about every wedded couple.

Of course, to know so much one must go to a great deal of trouble, and Frau Quiebus was on the move all day, every day. The town shook beneath her steps, and many people trembled before her.

Frau Quiebus's late spouse, a very small, droll fellow, had been a pharmacist. He had discovered a surefire remedy for consumption, put up in convenient pills to be taken three times a day fifteen minutes before each meal, found amazingly effective by God-knows-what doctor—and definitely not cheap. A remedy, then, for the same cruel disease to which he himself succumbed several years later. His wife was left behind disconsolate and very well-off. "The gods," she was accustomed to say, "give their darlings all things on earth, all of the joys, infinite joys, and all of the sorrows, infinite sorrows." I recall very well once watching this

55

powerful woman carry her little husband over a puddle as if he were a doll.

She had two children. She had Edwin, whose health was her constant care, and Carola, the sunshine of her life, who, besides the Powenz family, was the only creature in all Moessel with secrets to which Frau Quiebus was not privy.

"Carola tells me everything. She really is such a child in these matters," explained Frau Quiebus everywhere she went, referring to matters of love.

Carola was, moreover, a tall, pretty girl, a strawberry blonde with a talcum-powder complexion, innocent eyes and the loveliest legs; for the latter she once won a substantial prize, without her mother's knowing anything about it, of course, in an advertising contest sponsored by a stocking manufacturer—and that despite strong international competition. Carola had, you see, a magnificent body, a fact of which her mother made no secret, seeing that it was much like her own when she was young.

Edwin, however, was a good boy and very obedient. By nature he would have been quite healthy, had not Frau Quiebus been so continually concerned about him. She was very proud of what she thought was her keen eye in recognizing sickness—especially sickness in Edwin.

"I can see plain as day you're feverish. Be a good boy now and go take your temperature,"

Frau Quiebus would say. And her son obeyed, even though he felt perfectly well. He even had to put up with enemas, for his mother was convinced that all illness—whether stomachache, headache, flu, rheumatism or even melancholy, anger or love itself—doubtless had its origin in bad bowels. Poor Edwin was forever "looking dreadful again today." And something had to be done about it.

The family physician was Doctor Flaum, of whom Frau Quiebus said in some embarrassment that she would not let him examine her for anything in the world, for she found him "really much too attractive for that." Because the lad was a bit constipated, Doctor Flaum suggested a daily morning massage with a cast-iron ball about the size of a fist, and since otherwise it would be too cold, this was then covered in red-checked flannel. "Roll that ball," the doctor prescribed, and thirteen-year-old Edwin rolled it. Every morning when he awoke, and before breakfast, just as ordered, the lad would take the ball in his sleepy hands and let it slide back and forth over his white belly—at first reluctantly, but later with real fervor, having sensed a strange yet pleasant feeling within him to which he yielded more and more.

Doctor Flaum was indeed a handsome man, pale as fear itself, with a noble hopelessness to his features; he was a physician who took all illness, be it the sniffles or a disease like cancer (Frau Quiebus

Dr. Flaum, G.P.

always said "cahncer"), equally seriously —that is, if the patient ever really got a chance to describe his symptoms. For right off he would find himself interrupted. "Strange," Doctor Flaum would say, "I've got exactly the same thing myself." His own symptoms were a little worse, to be sure; in fact, they were unbearable. He could hardly stand the constant pain in the lower back that radiated clear up into his shoulders; and he would complain in moving detail of how terrible it was to be so fatigued and listless. Until finally, the compassionate patient, perhaps himself as dangerously ill as droll Herr Quiebus had once been, would begin to feel sorry for the doctor and would suggest that he might want to try an extract of holly leaves and juniper berries, drunk hot just before bedtime, or maybe the old time-tested remedy of hot mudpacks for the entire body. And then how full of gratitude was Doctor Flaum, how deeply consoled he felt on departure. And, full of pity for the poor fellow, the patient died content.

Charity, morality, patriotism and piety were Frau Quiebus's most conspicuous qualities. Her charity balls were as famous as her tact in matters of the heart. She admitted to what in her own funny way she called an almost immorally passionate devotion to the kaiser. "Isn't he handsome, isn't he just *too* handsome!" she would cry whenever she showed a visitor her edifying collection of pictures of the kaiser. "Just think," she would confess amid her tears, "not long ago I dreamt about him all dressed up in his uniform, and he kissed me on the brow!" Like him, she loved to hold little worship services for her domestic servants.

And in contrast, the Powenzes—parasites, debauchees, godless folk with no respect for authority! Such antitheses make it only too apparent why Frau Quiebus said in disgust, "Filth and Powenzes are the two things that can turn my mood to one of profoundest sorrow."

It had been officially proven beyond any doubt that for some time now the Powenzes had been living on pilfered electrical current. They had secretly tapped a lead-in wire somewhere and were thus getting free light, paid for by the town as a whole. But what did they own that the town could put a lien on? Their destitution was well established.

As a result of the town's suspicions—kept ever alive by the enemy, Quiebus and Gockeley— the Powenzes understandably encountered all kinds of unpleasantness: interrogations, searches and surveillance by the police. The Powenz pack only got worried when totally innocent, so they took with enthusiasm to these police visits and succeeded in transforming even the most harmless affair into a grand scene. Their native talent for very effective tableaux and for theatrics in general made it possible for them to produce little impromptu comedies on any occasion.

At the appearance of the police officers, the little ones would hurl themselves sobbing around their mother's neck, while their father would sit at the table, his arms hanging limply at his sides, his eyes staring vacantly ahead, the completely broken man. Jadup, in the role of the ingenuous child, asked in his most charming voice, "Mother dear, what do these mean men want? They won't hurt us, will they?" They called out cues to one another, and their hearts filled with rapture when something went off particularly well. Now they would be all wounded pride, now they would intentionally incriminate themselves. In short, they played their parts so masterfully that in the end they were unassailable.

The very precociousness of the boys gave one pause. It was not very nice of them, but they thought it a great joke to make the pharmacist or virtuous barber blush by discreetly purchasing certain items.

Ever curious about matters of love and death, Jadup took pleasure in such childish impudence. Of an evening he loved to lie in wait for the servant girls and watch them with their sweethearts, and he soon knew all the tender love affairs in Moessel, both their strengths and weaknesses. When on Sundays the recruits would walk hand in hand through the woods, he would follow them secretly, and he was soon the terror of all nature-loving couples. He was a depraved boy, good-looking and insolent, extremely cruel and loved with an almost ineffable love by many of his schoolmates on account of his unnatural, supernatural charm.

It was whispered about—and I consider it perfectly possible—that one of them drowned himself because Jadup had cast him off, and that Jadup, with both horror and a smile on his face, burned the farewell letter that revealed the sad cause of it all. No one guessed that one night this awful boy broke into the chamber where the corpse lay so that he could shine a flashlight on the face of the unfortunate lover just to see what it looked like. He was that fearless. And later, his was to be perhaps the most cruel fate ordained for any of the Powenzes.

But as a matter of fact, they got along with the police quite well. The family always felt especially secure with an officer or two around.

Chapter Ten

*In which the subject is the physical deformity
and the mad behavior of the mighty Kaspar*

That the family's reputation was so bad,
however, can be traced chiefly to Kaspar's dubious
achievements.

It has already been reported that even as a
young lad he managed some most astonishing
things in matters of love. The rumor that by some
quirk of nature he had been gifted with a double
dose of virility was never fully laid to rest, perhaps
because it was indeed true, perhaps because this
bit of fantasy originated in Violand's whimsical
brain and, for reasons of fraternal chauvinism, he
thought it would not hurt to confide to his highly
amazed schoolmates that the story was only too
true. At any rate, Kaspar was envied and cursed
for his luck with the ladies by all the slaves of love
in Moessel.

Following his love affair with the girl from a
most respectable home (to wit: the aforemen-
tioned Anna Fehling who had poured out her
heart to Frau Quiebus), Kaspar loved classy Elsa
Kapf, the highly sought after daughter of the proc-

tor of Moessel Academic High. After her, delicate and lovely Akelie, a girl whose home was Stralsund and who only visited Moessel temporarily. And then he loved two twin sisters, Renata and Regina Zobel, two exceedingly industrious and amorous lacemakers from the nearby town of Reihersham. He was never able to forget the experience, though it was but one among a thousand others. For these two young ladies seemed to have been personally instructed in the most charming passionate arts by the god of love himself. Kaspar therefore returned to them both more than once thereafter. Nevertheless, he left them for somber and unquenchable Abigail, the daughter of a carnival exhibitor; and then he left her for her girl friend, yet another Anna by the way, the most jealous creature he had ever met. She did not last long, particularly because one afternoon he was detained after school at the home of his penmanship teacher, Herr Jorkum, and there met his young wife. At first she laughed at him, and then she fell completely under his spell for almost a full year. It was a period filled with danger, indiscretion and the strangest rendezvous behind the back of that very strict teacher, nor was it without consequences. Hermine Kirchner was the next. Actually she had a secret crush on Kaspar's brother Fabian, and Kaspar was permitted to come to her only in the guise, so to speak, of Fabian, who was amazed that when Kaspar went out, he sometimes wore his, that is to say, Fabian's, clothes. Then Kaspar loved Melanie, the first girl to deceive *him* before he cheated on *her*. He found that very amusing. Then, as far as I can ascertain, he loved a farm girl named Barbara or Babette from the village of Rothenbuehl, an affair not without its dangers, since the enraged village boys tried to waylay him. After her, came the refined and well-read Frau Katharina von Uhlenkamp,[6] whose husband at that point was off leading a very important scientific expedition in North Africa. Kaspar loved them all, and more besides, and hardly a one of them held a grudge against him. And some called him back again and again, despite all the others. Kaspar kept an exact catalogue of his amours, which is now in the archives of the Powenz Museum. Some photographs of the ladies are included. Permission to examine it, however, is granted only for scientific purposes.

But we can ban to the realm of fable the following scurrilous tale as the monstrous brainchild of an overheated and excessively prurient imagination (of the sort that, unfortunately, many a Moesseler may call his own).

---

[6]One should note how Kaspar hoped in this way to introduce Powenzian blood into old established, influential families. I shall perhaps return to this fact later.

I am speaking of that wild intermezzo when Kaspar unknowingly and inadvertently dallied with one of the secret mistresses of his father, with the deceitful Juliane, a pale-skinned and wicked creature whose mouth made fools of men—one of them Kaspar, who fell deeply in love with her. Now it is alleged that, as she was trifling with the love-sick Kaspar in the woods one day, his father appeared upon the scene, having tracked them down. It is said he grabbed the lad like a tomcat by the nape of the neck, dragged him out of the bushes and bound him to the nearest fir tree—and then, both to torture and instruct, let him watch.

Kaspar had never seen such powerful, primal lovemaking, such rip-roaring, bearish tenderness. He cursed, he cheered. He is said wisely never to have approached any more Julianes. It is only with the gravest reservations that I mention this abominable rumor.

Kaspar's amorous adventures could not long remain undiscovered in Moessel. He was therefore compelled to leave Academic High shortly before graduation. The evidence against him was too overwhelming. Above all, he had been impudent enough to make advances to the principal's daughter, until then a blameless and shy child who, when separated from Kaspar forthwith—as was only proper—wept bitterest tears. (Today she is a well-known film actress with fond memories of Kaspar.) Frau Quiebus did not shrink from getting involved in this mess, in the hope that as the result of her efforts the youth of Moessel might not be poisoned in the future by this profligate. She gave a nasty scolding to little Frau Powenz, who merely replied, "You watch over your own chicks. I'll let my ganders run!"

Chapter Eleven

Concerning love of one's neighbor

Arather violent explosion of stored fire-works—recklessly endangering the inhabitants of the building, setting Heinrich's red hair on fire and leaving ugly scars from the burns—resulted in father Powenz's being given notice yet again.

The procession was once more notably festive, ending this time at the so-called Elephant House at 44 Kasimir Strasse. This was a three-story, red brick building with a stylish slate roof inscribed in white tile with the date of erection and the builder's initials; it looked as if it had been lopped off on both sides, like the last piece left of a cake. There it stood pretentiously between its modest neighbors. The two flanks were windowless. The vacant walls were used for advertising, and it was from a smirking elephant who raised a velocipede high in his trunk that the house took its name. On the other side, a gigantic pink baby with a perennial smile perennially drank Van Houten's cocoa.

In those days an eccentric by the name of

Knust lived in the house, and the Powenz pack all too often abused his guileless good nature to play him all kinds of naughty practical jokes. For Knust was a poet. From his hand we have a history of Moessel in humorous couplets, which he published at his own expense, and several grand pageants in iambic pentameter based on indigenous epic material.

Powenz, wicked man that he was, had advised him most urgently to publish these high-class poetical works, as he called them, and offered to relieve their author, ecstatic at such praise, of the bothersome and time-consuming task of printing—for a minimal fee, of course. It was Powenz as well who saw to it that, despite meticulous proof-reading by the author, several quite ludicrous misprints found their way into the text at the very last minute.

Knust lived on the third floor of the Elephant House; the second floor was occupied by the three superannuated Geist sisters, Katharina, Ernestina and Babette, who were also the owners of the building. They were notorious crepehangers and would frighten the nervous Moesselers with gloomy prophecies of death, which really did come to pass. Without ever being asked, they would say to someone straight out: you will die on such and such a day, at such and such a time; and there were people who did not think it so very pleasant to know such things.

All Moessel was astonished that the weird crones, with their sore red eyes and cold hands, with their slack, wicked mouths like monkeys and their continually runny noses—that these jaundiced birds of ill omen would rent the ground floor to the Powenz pack, of all people. They did it, however, on purpose, precisely because they utterly despised the Powenzes. They had lured them into the house, as it were, so as to be that much more sure of their destruction. And it was only after some time that the Powenzes, who were usually so shrewd, actually noticed that the ceilings had been bored through in several places and that the old witches had been watching and eavesdropping at will on the unsuspecting family. Violand, however, waited until just the right moment when ancient, rheumy-eyed Katharina was about to bend down over her peephole, to give her an efficacious squirt right in the face with a jet of Standard Imperial German indelible ink. Jadup, for his part, revenged himself on spinster Babette—who always got herself up like a teenager with powder, rouge and a flirty smile that revealed her revolting gray, rotten teeth—by filling her listening ear with wasps. And Fabian gave curious Ernestina such an improper eyeful that she decided it would be better to do no more spying from here on in.

The three Geist sisters

Chapter Twelve

Describes a family council
with musical accompaniment

One year before the World War, an event occurred that, though public opinion, as is its wont, thought it common enough and of no importance, proved in this case to have effects that were to be felt for years afterwards.

Powenz submitted to the Municipal Building Authority a petition (and it was in every respect an unexceptionable petition, a perfect model of good form) for a permit to build a villa on a lot on Luisen Strasse—that is, in the very finest neighborhood—directly across from the home of Frau Quiebus. The reader is already in large measure familiar with the history behind this petition, which was here accompanied by a battery of detailed blueprints of the full view, the floor plan and various elevations.

Powenz's brick collection had prospered and flourished, his brave lads were earning money, and he could think seriously of turning the first spadeful of earth—if not immediately, at least very soon. The first right of purchase for the lot had been secured, and that it lay directly across from Frau Quiebus's house gave the entire project a loftier purpose still.

Before Powenz had taken this decisive step, however, he had solemnly called his wife, his dear sons and his lovely daughter together for a family council, upon the outcome of which he wished to base his decision.

The invitation, issued one morning just before the daily thrashing, was received by the whole family with loudly bellowed applause.

According to the report of the county meteorologist, it was a rainy Sunday and, moreover, their father's birthday. The common sitting room was at once transformed by the sons' maneuvering the crates to form a kind of meeting hall or parliament. For reasons of solemnity, it was decided they would all remain in their shirts, that is, in long, quasi-sacerdotal nightgowns, which at once guaranteed a certain intimacy of mood. Powenz praised the cheerful zeal of his sons and distributed cigarettes, pretzels, wieners and wine, the latter being, after all, a weakness of his.

The meeting was held behind closed shutters to preserve strictest secrecy, and the sole illumination came from an oily, dusty kerosene lamp of frosted glass, fashioned to resemble a tightly corseted lady with a white parasol, an object that strangely enough never got smashed—a thing with good luck. There are such.

They sat there now around the lamp and, first things first, ate a hearty breakfast.

The Powenz pack all had chewing apparatuses that were strong, hard and extraordinarily well-developed anatomically. With the possible exception of the squeamish Heinrich, who ate no meat, the boys were in no way finicky. When later on, after having been repeatedly extended a gruff but cordial invitation by all the Powenzes, I did remain at table with them on occasion (though, I admit, only on Lilith's account), I myself was a witness to the unforgettable repasts that were customarily held among them.

I do not wish in the least to imply that the food at the Powenz table was bad, most certainly not. But it was always somewhat coarse. My stomach at any rate could never quite digest it. Perhaps this was owing to the fact that, since I might be called something of a lyrical eater, I found my appetite somewhat impaired, though never really spoiled, by the exuberance of epicurean gusto, by the sensual pleasure exhibited in tasting, devouring and slurping, above all as these acts were performed by father Powenz, whom in all other respects I revere even to this day, by mighty Kaspar and by slender but voracious Zephirin. The Powenzes did not eat, they feasted. Those large mouths, really quite pretty under normal conditions of chatting, laughing or sleeping, could encompass amazing quantities all at once. They chewed with their cheeks stuffed full. They cracked and crushed the bones of roast poultry between their jaws—and it happened every now and again that a chicken ran right under the wheels of one of the boys' bikes. Noodles dripping with fat hung like icicled beards down over their chins. The muscles of their faces swelled and kept time with the chewing. They devoted themselves totally to the all-important pulverization of foodstuffs.

They slurped with ahs! and hmms! When they talked, it was only with their mouths full, and then only in praise of the food. They would toss scraps of bread in the air and catch them in their wide open mouths. They smacked their lips noisily, a cacophony of tones. And it was all, I admit it, a bit too much for me. When Powenz spread the butter on his bread so that it squirted and oozed in all directions, it was almost a cultic act, though a rather rudimentary one, to be sure. When eating, his countenance resembled that of an artist totally immersed in his work. In a word, he ate intensely, thinking all the while, it seemed, of the waving golden fruits of the field, nor forgetting the milk cow, that sacred beast, nor the milkmaid at her churning. To all appearances, eating made him think of beautiful, edifying things.

And so now, gathered round their homely lamp, they sat uncombed, heartily feasting, drinking, smoking, all to the glory of God.

The father rose at last, the first to do so as was only proper, his tattooed breast partially bared to reveal the house that was all his dream. There were the blue trees with their almost natural foliage of reddish chest hair, and above them like a cloud, the beard that framed Powenz's face, hot and radiant with wine. He held his thick cigar upright and for a while it seemed he was speaking only to the smoke rising from it, as if to some spirit that he had conjured up. Every now and then he would puff out his cheeks and raise his chin, convulsively repressing a belch. His argument was as follows:

"Beloved members of my family, and you above all, my dear sweet courageous wife, tireless custodian of the fragile lamp of domestic bliss, hearken to me. I have bid you come together to take counsel on a matter that lies, I may say, near to all our hearts. Moreover, this matter can now be said, I believe, to be developing rather nicely."

Powenz cleared his throat and resumed his grand oration.

"This morning, while you were all yet lying enfolded in Morpheus's tender arms, your father had long been up, out ambulating through the fresh dewy countryside round about Moessel and thinking to himself that perhaps the new day had some gift in store for him. And lo, it had indeed!" At these words Powenz held out a brick in front of him as if it were a book, gazing down at it benevolently. "What is this? A brick. Nothing more. It lay there heedless upon the path, a shelter to beetles and centipedes. A brick, nothing more. But to me it means more than that," (with voice upraised) "for it is a part of that great whole so near to all our hearts.

"I mean our house. I still am touched to think of how our sensitive son Heinrich as a child once laid such a brick in the earth like a seed, and watered it diligently in the belief that a house would grow from it. But nothing grew. Ah yes, it is not all that simple.

"I am an old, footloose wanderer. And yet, some seventeen years ago now, it may even be eighteen, as once again I entered the inhospitable town where first I saw the light of day, I decided: it is good to be here, here will I put down my roots. Since that day I have been gathering brick upon brick. This one bears the number 999 and a date, both inscribed by my own hand. Put it with the others."

Lilith rose, received the brick and bore it solemnly on opened palms to the appointed place.

"Lie there among thy brothers until we have need of thee for a house. But, you ask quite rightly,

77

why *here.* For there is a proverb in these parts that says: Everywhere else is better than Moessel. And I answer," (Powenz's voice took on a stirring ring) "I was homesick for Moessel from whence I came."

"It makes me want to cry," Heinrich interrupted with a sob.

"Such a noble eruption of emotion," Powenz continued, pouring himself some wine, "does you honor. It speaks well for your heart!

"I have not always had it easy in life. Life has not been exactly a bed of roses. And nevertheless —life, life, and I for my part do not hesitate to love it with all the passion of my heart and soul, life is—now, how shall I express it?—it is, well, splendid, simply splendid! No, Heinrich do not shake your head, gentle lad, shake it not.

"*Life,* I say, is splendid, indeed it is! But *living,* living is ghastly, miserable, undignified, dreary. I have, as you my beloved family know, always held fast to the opinion (though, sad to say, I am alone in holding it), to the opinion that at present mankind has fallen victim to an error concerning this splendid life. There is no need for cynical smiles, little Jadup," Powenz said, stopping to knock off his cigar ash onto the lad's head. "In its madness, mankind has put living where life should be. That is the error that afflicts all of us, yes, all; the error against which you and I, my loved ones, do battle with all our soul. And this is the crucial factor, we

battle with some success—at least for us." (Bravo!)

Powenz paused here briefly, letting these last words take full effect. As is customary among students, the boys drummed on their crates and stamped their feet, and Powenz made an obliging bow. Then motioning for silence with his large right hand, its shadow towering up behind him like the shadow of a giant, Powenz proceeded to describe in a chatty, informal way how his old idea of a house of his own was now approaching its realization.

Countless wonderful bricks, he joked, were pining away, just waiting to be mortared together by constructive and loving hands.

"It is a grand goal, an ideal for which I would at any time and with greatest pleasure offer up this tattered thing I call my life."

And with these terrifying words, Powenz drank deeply; and then, nodding gratefully to the wine and sucking at the moist tips of his moustache, he wiped his mouth with relish and, despite Sabina's protestations that his life be preserved for her and the children's sake, repeated his statement, "As I said, it would be my greatest pleasure! The handle to that mysterious door lies ever in my hand. I need only fling it open."

Powenz picked up a knife from the crate and set it pathetically to his breast.

"Hail to thee, o great darkness, o eternal silence—receive me unto thee!"

And as Heinrich cried out in full horror, "Good heavens! He won't hurt himself, will he?" he replied almost politely, "Oh no, wouldn't think of it. But now to return to the house.

"All we need," he said almost unconcernedly in closing, "all we need is money! But money is of no importance, can be of no importance in life. I resolutely ignore it!" (Well, well, well!)

"Nevertheless, I have summoned you, my own flesh and blood. Just as we are, we, the Powenz pack, are a power in the world, no mere nation, but rather like an empire. We are, if you will, a sovereign power. Yes, we are that. And we are feared.

"But we are something else as well. We ourselves are living, breathing capital! I have always taken the firm position that one should never be more deeply in debt than is absolutely necessary.

"By means of a small encroachment upon our future reserves, I have succeeded in liquidating our debts almost entirely—all except for a few small obligations owed the baker, butcher and, if I am not mistaken, the grocer (plus, perhaps, a small sum due Adam's Wineshop and a few others). I therefore move that the house, whose most essential parts, by which I mean the bricks, are now more or less ready at hand, that our house be built with all deliberate speed!"

Toward the end, Powenz had spoken with prophetic confidence. In his beard hung the very

The Elephant House
The Powenz pack lived on the second floor
from 1912 to 1924

dew of speech. He stood there with disheveled hair, glowing with ardor. His body warmed the room.

His wife and children were at one in their awareness that Powenz was an exceptional, yes, that he was an absolutely splendid man.

Following this important speech by their father, the first to take the floor was, surprisingly, gentle Heinrich.

Heinrich was rather different from all his brothers. He was delicate and pensive by nature. His powers of imagination were not so gay and reckless as, for instance, those of blithely lazy Fabian, whom he envied, but neither were they any less extravagant than those of the other Powenzes—they were simply more ominous. His face was a bit too small, or appeared to be so because his ears were so large, seeming always to listen in terror for distant evil, because his eyes were always opened so wide and because his large, pale, melancholy nose was set out from it as if just waiting to be grabbed. His mouth was fixed as if he wanted to utter an eternal "oh." He always blushed at others' misdeeds, and he was ever ready, as the alleged perpetrator, silently to suffer their punishment for them. He often worried whether the baker across the street would be able to sell all his rolls before they turned stale, and whether the peddler could hawk her vegetables before they wilted. He believed, in all seriousness, in justice on earth. When on a train, he would compulsively tell stories about train accidents. He would turn white if someone merely whispered the word "war," but would then discourse for hours on end about what sorts of wounds a soldier might incur out on the battlefield, describing them all in vivid detail from head to toe, while shivering at the grisly visions that forced themselves upon him.

"Oh," he once said when the conversation turned to marriage, "oh, if you could only know for sure which girl providence truly meant for you to have. Because, after all, it can only be just one, I'm certain. But assuming I lived in Africa or in America, isn't it possible that I might just as well fall in love with someone there, thinking that she was the only one and...

"Or when you choose a profession, just look what that's like. Let's assume I want to be a hair-dresser, for instance; who can say but what I might have been a general, and..."

He concluded almost every sentence with "and," but never followed through. It was absolutely awful when he had to write a letter, for then he would smile with the torture of racking his brain for that first word—the choices were indeed infinite.

"And," Heinrich now began in his soft voice, while his reddish-brown eyes fringed with white lashes were opened wide in dumb terror like those of a young calf. "Oh, father, oh, mother, and you, my lovely sister, and you, dearest brothers, just stop and consider what such a house would mean. A house, so square and hard, and built on an unviolated plot of earth, where nothing ever stood before—is that not a brutal invasion of the atmosphere, is that not arbitrary despotism and... The bricks, are they not dried earth made infertile forever? Are the beams and boards not murdered trees? Does not the spade with every cut wantonly destroy our brother the earth as he lies there? Does not every step we take purposelessly and carelessly destroy life that was so long in the making? For instance, such cunning creatures as the worm, the ant and the ladybug? Oh, everything is so random and haphazard and..."

Heinrich stood with one finger raised in warning as if he had something more to say. He shook his head slowly in disapprobation.

The family fell silent in awkward embarrassment.

"He's some degeneration in the stock," Baltus muttered, "or could it be, Sabina, that you...?"

"Herr Powenz, what an ugly suspicion!" the good woman cried.

"Forgive me, love," old Powenz said, and her children comforted her as well. It had only been his little joke.

Finally Violand stood up, laying his hand on Heinrich's shoulder, who actually still had much he wanted to say, but Violand gave him an amiable look and saw to it that he seated himself. Now he sprang up onto the crate where he had been sitting and spoke forcefully and with expansive gestures.

"To tell the truth, ladies and gentlemen, people do not want us here in Moessel. We enjoy, it seems, a considerable lack of popularity. We are undesirables. In a word: we think for ourselves and that upsets people. And precisely for that reason, I second father's motion. The house must be built. It shall be built, it shall!"

Father Powenz, who in the course of Heinrich's distressing speech had drunk heavily, raised himself up fully and said, "Well done, my son. That is what I call a fine speech. The house shall be built, yes, yes it shall! Even if it means that I must swear from this solemn moment on never to let another drop of heavenly wine pass these lips, not another drop, never again! Yea, I renounce wine, and should I break my oath, you may..."

But at once his sons sprang up in unison and encircled their father:

"No, good Baltus," they cried with something approaching tenderness, "no, dear father and splendid citizen, do not do that. Drink. Drink and may you ever enjoy it!"

"What sons I have!" said Powenz with sincerest fervor.

"This is the most beautiful hour of my life," Sabina whispered.

Many more things were discussed, above all the augmentation of income necessary to finance their intentions. To this end, Jadup wickedly suggested that Kaspar might easily charge each of his girl friends a small fee.[7]

Fabian proposed that they form a traveling circus, seeing it would be no problem for each of them to participate. They finally agreed, however, that there was perhaps more money to be made if each would perform on his own and in ostensible competition with the others. This meant that they would move in on unsuspecting villages and market towns in the region from all sides at once, i.e., divide and conquer. The idea was to act as the replacement for a whole county fair, with bellicose ballads like "Sock it to Him, Sam," with a little menagerie, with Lilith as a gypsy fortune-teller and their father as harpist. Violand would do his magic act, and even lazy Fabian agreed to perform as a mathematical whiz-kid if they promised him a bedroom of his own in the new house. Zephirin decided to work as a silhouette artist, while their

[7]And why not?

good mother modestly suggested that she could perhaps sell balloons.

All these efforts were for the sake of the house.

They drank and talked till evening. At about six o'clock, father Powenz's customary hour of melancholy, he expressed a longing that they make music together. At once the treasured instruments were let down from the ceiling; they propped their music against the wine bottles, tuned up in melodic confusion and then, their cold and sloppy cigars dangling and swaying from their mouths, made splendid music.

Powenz counted time out loud and once wept a bit. Then they played Beethoven's Fifth, using Fabian's ingenious arrangement for the Powenz orchestra, which, to be sure, he had been able to complete only under strictest supervision to prevent him from falling asleep on the job.

And so it would have been a truly fine evening, had not Jadup made an awful fluff in the last movement. This resulted in an exchange of words, and then of blows. The two ladies only barely succeeded in raising the endangered instruments out of the way once the battle had commenced.

Willful Jadup lunged violently at his father, who grabbed him about the waist and lifted him in the air, shouting that he would teach him to raise a hand against the man who had so benevolently begotten him. Zephirin flung heavy seaweed pillows from the top bunks down onto his father's wrathful head, and Violand moved in behind a shield of piled-up pillows and with a rapid thrust ripped his father's shirt in two, revealing the bluish scenes on his shoulders beneath. Kaspar wrestled in proper Greco-Roman style with the bellowing old man, whose legs were held tight by Fabian and who stoically endured annoying but harmless blows to his face. Heinrich did not fight, but stood off to one side, scolding in his soft, mournful voice. He called them all scalawags and scoundrels. The ghostly shadows of the warriors danced about the room.

Only Lilith came to her father's aid, revenging herself on her brothers for the many humiliations she had suffered at their hands. She waded into them, biting, scratching, spitting like a preposterous fury, her mahogany hair, cut in a boy's bob, flapping at the edges of her enraged face. She bared her teeth and gave a wrathful "grrr!" At that moment, her father managed to grab two of his sons, Kaspar and Violand, by their shirts, pulling the cloth up over their heads, so that they could not see a thing and in their blindness began to lambaste one another. Jadup and Zephirin broke into loud laughter, and even the guardian of the lamp, their mother, smiled.

The battle was over.

Baltus Powenz (X) with the author
on the occasion of his seventieth birthday

They now talked at length about their own new house, about how big it would have to be and about the garage and the tennis courts. They came up with all sorts of fabulous ideas.

Fabian, for example, seemed to talk in his sleep as he described his ideal room, one where you could reach everything from the bed. And he made it all sound so comfortable and luxurious, that in no time every single Powenz had fallen asleep, a smile on his lips.

For a while Violand stood there among the sleepers, directing the concert of snores, muting a tone here, calling up a forte there.

BOOK OF
TRIBULATIONS

Man's greatest enemy is man!

—*Baltus Powenz*
Porcupinions

Chapter One

In which presumption is quite properly
squashed but then refuses to take it lying down

As a result of this memorable family council,
Baltus Powenz requested permission to build his
house, and his petition would probably have been
granted without further ado, had it not been submitted by quite such a disreputable citizen.

Herr Gockeley exploded.

"Where," he shouted, "where did that man
ever get the money to build a house? Not by honest means, I'll bet."

And he decided to bring to bear all the influ-
ence he had, which was not a little, to defeat such
an outrageous request. This was properly a matter
for the Municipal Housing Authority, and approval of the plans was primarily dependent on the
decision of the town surveyor, Herr Knipfel, a
very powerful man in Moessel.

Knipfel was virtually bald, but he had learned
the knack of training a single strand on one side of
his fringe so that it was long enough to be combed
as a brilliantined bridge across his shiny pate; true,
it did not entirely hide the bareness, but at least it

bisected it. The reflective surface was lent added interest by the presence of several moles and warts.

In terms of his face, it must be noted that Knipfel's expression unfortunately betrayed a most unattractive trait. Knipfel's constant worry was that he might starve. For this reason, he customarily ate little lunches late at night, and there is ample evidence that he also carried emergency rations with him, year in, year out, like a soldier out on maneuvers. He suffered from a voracious appetite, and malicious tongues maintain that he once accosted a small schoolboy who was just about to take a hearty bite of his chive and butter sandwich, snatched it right out of his mouth and devoured it before the eyes of the wailing child. Such a direful appetite had given his face a gluttonous aspect; the lips were greasy and always in motion. His nose was pressed down on his upper lip, sniffing constantly, and in size and form it resembled a fetal pig. And yet Knipfel was not very fat at all—except that his belly protruded like a firm, plump ball.

Knipfel's buildings were what gave the new part of town its distinctive appearance, and his taste in matters artistic had been decisive for Moessel. The salient feature of his architecture was its foundation in tried and true designs out of the past. Thus Moessel could boast that it possessed exquisite replicas of many world-renowned structures. The slaughterhouse had been built in noble Renaissance style and the insane asylum in serene Baroque, while the new crematorium was Byzantine. Moreover, these buildings had one advantage over their famous originals—they were all brand-new. If that can be called an advantage, for Knipfel saw it in quite a different light. Experience had shown that a new house done in Gothic style was ugly, but that an old moss-covered one looked grand and romantic. Thanks to Knipfel's foresight, then, new buildings were provided with a kind of artificial mildew right from the start; they were, one might say, built old, much to everyone's satisfaction. Moessel also had him to thank for the suggestion that a marble monument (sculpted by Bernauer) be erected in honor of the unfortunate Queen Luise, even though that noble lady had never once set foot in Moessel—as proven incontestably by Valentin Knust in his brief history of the town. The monument is mentioned in Baedeker's guide. Unfortunately, every year, from October till April, it must be protected against the elements by a shed of bare wooden planks.

The new Moessel Town Hall, a neo-Gothic structure two years in the building (1899–1901), is Knipfel's work. It has a magnificent facade, but some drawbacks as well. In about half the rooms, the lights must be kept on all day, summer and winter, because the windows were designed small for stylistic reasons. The interior is, sad to say, gloomy and not at all inviting. In addition, the intricate lettering used on all the richly carved doorplates, on the marriage bureau for example, are completely illegible to the layman.

The so-called council chamber is a cold, sun-less room with hard, sharp-edged oaken chairs whose heavy ornamentation and slatted backs collect great quantities of dust. It was there that the housing authority gathered for the meeting that proved to be of such paramount importance for the course of our story.

Mayor Dattel, a kindly man in his fifties and a great mollifier of passions, opened the meeting at 10:45 A.M., arguing more or less as follows:

"Gentlemen, certain persons of my acquaint-ance, I might almost say, as it were, persons with whom I am on the friendliest terms, have called my attention to the fact that our town—and it is the welfare and prosperity of our dear Moessel, the ancient Moselinum of Roman times, which I must always hold before my eyes, which is ultimately my responsibility, and I feel that responsibility most deeply, I assure you—that our town, then, harbors within its walls a certain personage, of whom I do not hesitate to say—and I beg you, please, to regard what I shall now say as absolutely confidential—of whom I would not want to hesi-tate to say that one could very well feel tempted to describe him, and not without some disquiet, as a personage of Catiline mentality. You all know of whom it is I speak. Said personage has submitted a petition for a building permit, and I must confess that in my judgment the chances that said petition will be granted are, at this time, quite slim. The petitioner's wish, however, to build a house is in itself hardly a reprehensible one, and it is for that reason and on that basis alone that I most warmly urge this matter upon you for your consideration, despite the fact that I am personally in no way reconciled to it. I would like now to call upon our town surveyor, Herr Knipfel, to advise us both from a technical and from an artistic point of view."

Herr Knipfel, who always smiled as if he felt personally flattered no matter what the topic of conversation, first sent his tongue on a meticulous, painfully writhing tour of his mouth in search of the remains of his most recent meal; then, rubbing his hands, he paid extensive tribute to the mayor's great services in matters architectural, but proceeded to add that he must now contradict the mayor, who had so warmly taken the part of the petitioner, although from a purely humane point of view he could, of course, understand the mayor only too well. He was unable, however, to reconcile this petition with his conscience as an artist; he must, in fact, for reasons of town-planning, refuse it straight out, even though the plans themselves unfortunately represented no breach of building and zoning codes. But this was no house, it was a cardboard cutout, a matchbox for ladybugs (laughter). If this petition were approved, he would resign. "All I have to add is: either—or! And," he concluded, "I mean what I say!"

Herr Gockeley explained in his best business-like manner that the neighbors, too, had raised serious objections, especially the universally respected Frau Quiebus. The lot on which this particular gentlemen wished to build his house was, moreover, a vital part of the town's recreational resources, one of the few remaining patches of green meant to ease the eyes, lungs and souls of urbanites. He really had nothing whatever against these folks, but...

The house Powenz planned had certainly been designed with utmost sobriety and economy. It was entirely devoid of ornament, since ornament costs money without adding beauty. It would indeed have been only a box or a cube had not windows and doors been provided for. The basic unit of measure, of course, was that dictated by the proportions of the standard brick.

The large workshoplike windows shown in the plans made the house look like a factory. But Powenz explained candidly that life itself was work enough for him and that his family was really just another business engaged in manufacturing another product, though an especially precious one: live human beings. In that sense, every house was a factory and ought, therefore, to look like one.

To be brief: the Powenz project was not approved. In that very same night—that is, before Powenz was in fact officially informed of this decision—[8] an unknown boy or boys smashed the windows of the homes of Messrs. Gockeley and Knipfel, as well as those of totally innocent citizens, and the stones were thrown with such accuracy that suspicion immediately fell on the Powenz boys.

The police, notified with all due speed, made a surprise raid before the night was over. They found the suspects sleeping peacefully, not a single one of them missing.

Morning's light also revealed that the noble marble figure of the martyred queen had likewise been most vilely defaced during the night, again by the hand of an unknown boy (or boys). She had been made up; her lips were painted red, ditto the cheeks, her eyebrows and lashes darkened, giving

---

[8]He had learned of it immediately through the well-organized Powenz Press Agency. Throughout the entire meeting, Violand had been sitting underneath the green table in the center of the room.

her a saucy, slightly disreputable look. And someone had taken the trademark of a local glove manufacturer, a large red-enameled tin glove, and pulled
it on over her hand.

Thus the curtain was raised on the great feud
between the Powenz pack and the intolerant
town, a feud that outlasted the World War.

It may be that certain legends have been
unfairly connected with the Powenz pack, because
now and again (or once, perhaps) they were indeed
entirely innocent. It is said that it was their hired
stooges who one day tore up the street at the
busiest intersection in the center of town, securing
the excavation in proper fashion by fencing it in
and, following police regulations, affixing red flags
to it by day and lanterns by night. The citizenry
patiently detoured around it, while a policeman
directed traffic, until several days later it was
discovered that the hole was totally unauthorized,
that it was only a successful attempt to harass the
town fathers. For everyone had taken that hole
seriously.

The Powenz pack steadfastly denied the deed
at the time. Not without envy, for they admitted
that it would have suited them just fine.

KNIPFEL

Herr Knipfel
Town Surveyor for Moessel on the Maar

Chapter Two

*In which the subject is boyhood bellicosity
and there is mention made of a she-panther*

The bloody Battle of the Boys on Red Ridge
(and by this name it is known even today among
the citizens of Moessel) should be seen as a natural
consequence of the insult implied in the rejection
of Powenz's petition. The underlying motive was
thus quite clear, and an immediate cause was soon
found.

The honor of initiating these hostilities—thus
marking the beginning of one of history's bitterest
wars ever fought by boys—fell to Violand during a
fifteen-minute school recess.

Violand was no commonplace fellow; he said
to himself that the customary jostling with one
shoulder and the traditional question, "Djuwan
sumpin?" (translated: Do you want something?)
would not suffice in this case. He therefore bought
a small bag of black cherries, took up a position
near the unsuspecting Emil Knipfel, and waited
patiently. He waited that is until Emil yawned,
whereupon he immediately spat three well-aimed
cherry pits into that mouth opened wide, much to

the queasy amusement of the other schoolboys in attendance.

Rosy-cheeked Emil Knipfel was, however, a fine, upstanding lad, by far the neatest and cleanest in his class and generally well-liked. He had a rare reputation for the strictest chastity in matters of body and soul. He did not blush, he blanched whenever Fabian told one of his gleefully crude jokes or when, with an air of naiveté, little Jadup favored his comrades with outrageous off-color anecdotes concerning the love life of the town. Spick-and-span Emil took no pleasure in such things, which was why to his utmost torment and to the coarse amusement of his schoolmates (versed as they were in vice), he was often the object of all sorts of indecent practical jokes. He would defend himself amidst such temptations in the most ridiculous and sorry fashion by threatening, for example, to tell his father—which he never did. He was a diligent but rather poor student, who, to the astonishment of his more godless neighbors, would fold his hands in prayer before every test. There was something almost uncanny about such piety, for his lips would murmur and his believing eyes would roll heavenwards. Despite which, he almost always got a C-minus.

It was indeed pitiful to observe Emil's fastidiousness when he met up with any sort of untidiness—how he would suffer from the smell of the classroom, wrapping himself in a fragrant fog of eau de cologne, how the poor lad shuddered before the broad blackberry pie smiles of the loutish Powenz boys with their wild, uncombed locks.

The effect, therefore, of Violand's cherry pits in Emil's mouth was especially dreadful. He felt very sick. His face was distorted, its color verging on green; nevertheless, he threw himself at the "Powenz rat," and momentarily in command of unnatural strength, succeeded in tumbling him to the ground. Fabian liberated his brother, while all around the schoolboys split into two groups, the Pit-spitters and the Knipflites, the former being considerably smaller in numbers, though the more seasoned warriors.

Among the Knipflites, the key positions were held by Edwin Quiebus, in whose pampered body there beat a courageous heart, pious Emil and the somewhat untrustworthy Helmut Gockeley, who looked just like his papa—receding chin, buckteeth, myopic eyes, scraggly blond hair and all.

This first skirmish in the schoolyard ended in a draw, having been prematurely halted by the intervention of the school janitor. Later, when classes were over, Jadup assumed the role of envoy and swinging a dirty white handkerchief knotted to his ruler, presented the Knipflites with a written declaration of war, challenging them to a showdown battle to be fought in Kyps Woods the following Saturday afternoon.

In a sultry clearing overgrown with raspberry brambles, thistles and blackthorn, a breeding ground for horseflies and hornets, where the air was filled with the odor of resin and dry heather, there was to be found the strategic point, a towering boulder of sandstone called Red Ridge. The sandstone had split open, and a white birch tree rose like a maypole up out of the moss and dirt-filled crevice.

This rock was the object of the battle; whoever could take it and hold it would be the victor. Both sides came well-armed. According to the canons of war then in effect, slingshots were legal, but only if chestnuts rather than stones were used as ammunition. Switches of acacia wood served as swords and spears. Shields were permitted. Kicking or tripping one's opponent was prohibited in hand-to-hand combat. Cavalry was very popular and consisted of having small, nimble, lightweight boys ride on the shoulders of the strongest and dumbest, who were steered by the ears or with punches. Jadup was considered an especially good equestrian.

The battle began rather unfavorably for the gentle folk when a three-boy patrol decided to be sly and creep up on the Powenz pack's rear as they were preparing for battle; instead, in a surprise attack by the even slyer Kaspar and Violand Powenz, they were taken captive—all except for one of them, who escaped to tell the sad tale.

The Powenzes had a flag displaying the symbol of a white house set against a red background.

Preceded by cavalry (six riders) and flanked by small patrol troops, their main force took the field of battle, feathered and painted like wild Indians and led by lazy Fabian, who had laid out the battle plan with mathematical precision.

The two prisoners were tied to a tree and were greatly tormented by the gnats and horseflies. It was very hot.

Entering the woods almost simultaneously, the two armies stood opposite one another, and what first began as universal shouts of contempt and bellicosity finally resolved itself into vehement and abusive speeches on the part of the two generals. War is war.

Fabian roared through his cupped hands, addressing the enemy as mama's boys, pansies and chickens, who, if they had any guts, would advance to attack, while Gockeley declared that he took the Powenzes for filthy riffraff, for scum and horse-apple collectors, who fouled the whole of nature with their stench—and then added other similar ungentlemanly turns of phrase.

On a nearby hill outside the combat zone, Baltus Powenz lay in his shirt sleeves beneath the shade of a beech tree, drinking wine and observing all this, at times raising an empty bottle to one eye, like some commander peering through his telescope. And how it did his paternal heart good to see his dear boys proven victorious. Later on, Sabina joined him, having been able to stand it no longer at home in this hour of danger. She could just as easily peel potatoes in the open air, she added, as if to excuse herself.

The Knipflites and Quiebusians were the first to gain the ridge, and they jubilantly took possession of it. In doing so, however, they weakened their advancing front line, and when Jadup attacked with his cavalry, he succeeded in driving the enemy riders from the field after only brief hand-to-hand combat.

At this juncture, one of the Powenzes' favorite weapons proved its superiority. They were armed with an apparatus they called the seven-tailed cat—seven supple leather thongs attached to a wooden handle; it was easy to hold and could be used to deliver decidedly painful blows to an opponent, especially to his hands.

Fabian now made good use of the ensuing confusion. Rapidly shifting some of his infantry, who fell upon the enemy with loud cries, he pressed the gentle folk off to one side; for tactical reasons they pulled back from their attackers with their line still intact, but they thereby left the way to Red Ridge open for Fabian. He was, however, greatly harassed by the long-range artillery of his opponents. Fabian's perky nose was already bloodied, and Heinrich was so plagued by horseflies, wasps and hornets that he was temporarily incapacitated.

"They've got better rubber in their slingshots," Fabian remarked. "They can shoot further. That means we have to move in for close combat."

And so once again it was Fabian's superior battle tactics that gave his side the advantage. He pulled back his right flank, wheeled around to the left and charged before Gockeley could see through the trick. He had been giving his orders from a well protected spot behind the rock, employing his full force against his enemy's right flank, so that now his left flank was forced to do battle with thin air, so to speak. This clever maneuver resulted in the gentle folk's withdrawing from the ridge, and in the course of this there occurred an event of unparalleled savagery.

Though he was by nature anything but pugnacious, being more inclined to read books, Edwin, with his fragile frame but valiant spirit, covered the retreat, or at least did all he could to cover it. He did this despite a splitting headache, for he could not bear strong sunshine, though he loved it more than anything else. There he stood now, dreadfully overheated, and held his ground, awkwardly and clumsily wielding a broken stick in his struggle with Violand, whose stinging blows whistled down on his hands and face. Edwin bore it all with tears of rage and pain, but he bore it. His shirt had been torn off, and red welts covered his sweating body. He took the blows, pitiable hero that he was, and neither budged nor yielded.

Such behavior, however, greatly annoyed Lilith, who, of course, had to be on hand, too.

She had eyebrows that grew together, that is, the hair of her right and left eyebrows touched just at the top of her nose. Some people say that means a person is passionate and sensual, others that he or she is humble of heart.

But in the battle between the Powenz pack and the gentle folk—as our friends disparagingly called the young scions of the Quiebus, Gockeley and Dattel families—fair Edwin personally experienced just how madly passionate and bloodthirsty Lilith could be. Heat and anger had whipped her to a frenzy. Emitting the ancient Powenz battle cry of "Waahoo!" she made a lunge for the despised weakling. But he let his hands fall to his sides.

"I do not strike women," he said with a sob.

Lilith then pounced on him like a wildcat, the claws of both hands bared, and she bit him angrily in the breast, just above his heart. There was blood on her teeth.

Battle of Red Ridge

Edwin let out a loud cry, grabbed her by the hair, tore her head away—and at last he took off. When he turned around once more, she was still there, her face twisted with rage. She had been watching him go, her claws still at the ready, her voice a low "grrr!"

I have intentionally said little about this savage creature thus far, for reasons that touch a sore point with me. For it is somewhat painful for an author to be derided by his readers as but one among the many lovers of his own heroine. It is especially painful in this case, since I have my doubts whether the author's role will prove a particularly laudable one.

Having managed to scrape through the early wretched years of childhood with much toil and trouble, Lilith was at first a regular monster. She was insufferable, always whining, always malicious and unspeakably ugly. She had kept her thin, whitish skin, beneath which her delicate veins were visible; of all the family members, she most resembled Heinrich, having the same reddish-brown bovine eyes and white eyelashes. These later are, as everyone knows, an abomination to a great many men.

Lilith was a tattletale; she scratched, she spat.

She was a nasty, sniveling little beast who took sick a couple of times a year. There is unhappy proof of her cruelty as a child; she once set about to make a dress of butterflies, catching them and sewing them, still alive, wing to wing. She preferred the little yellow ones, since she always looked especially good in yellow. She had no girl friends.

Only little by little did this clammy, bluish creature begin to take on color, particularly when her thin and sickly reddish hair began to be replaced by a thick, heavy growth the color of swamp water or, better—there is unfortunately no other way to put it—of the deep golden brown

From left to right: Emil Knipfel (seated)
Edwin Quiebus (standing)

of moist manure in the sunlight. Her complexion stayed white, but she lost the fishy look; she dried out, and the warmth of blood glowed in her cheeks. Her mouth was incomparable.

Many people maintain, however, that Lilith's face and head were a bit too large for her spare, straight body, that this gave her a kind of gnome-like, almost eerie look, so that no one could ever, ever love her.

Lilith's bestial attack proved decisive, and the battle ended in total defeat for the gentle folk. The mountain was taken by storm, though not without casualties. Zephirin, for instance, courageously climbed the birch tree, but the branch he was holding onto snapped and he fell, breaking his left arm. Violand had an ugly cut on his forehead, and his bloodied face was terrible to gaze upon. But it was only a scratch. Emil Knipfel just barely escaped and was very dirty. But Gockeley was taken prisoner, and he begged for mercy.

During the final phase of battle, father Powenz stood atop his hill, a giant of a man with his red-wine bottle raised in one hand, and fired the troops on, roaring "Hoho!" like a lion; whereas Frau Quiebus arrived on the scene waving her pink parasol and calling "Edwin" in a shrill voice. But Edwin had hidden himself. He was dabbing gingerly at his wounds, including Lilith's bite, which later left a quite visible scar.

The author, by the way, was a partisan of the

114

gentle folk. He was a member of that unlucky three-boy patrol and therefore unfortunately taken prisoner at the commencement of hostilities.

Zephirin later made use of his talents as an artist to depict from memory a very fine, multi-figured picture of the battle, seen, as it were, from the perspective of the gods (and to that extent perhaps not absolutely accurate), so that in just one picture he showed several important phases of the battle as occurring simultaneously in different places. The cannons and exploding grenades, however, are purely a product of his fertile imagination. Furthermore, the number of prisoners taken and of enemy banners captured in no way corresponds to reality.

And with a fine sense of tact, the young artist omitted reference to the unedifying scene of Lilith and Edwin. But at the sides, there are larger-than-life representations of Baltus Powenz with his wine bottle and Frau Quiebus with her parasol, both standing on billowy clouds like Homeric divinities supervising the battle. In the background lies the charming town of Moessel. Almost all the boys in the fray—none of them larger than tin soldiers—have a number next to them. On the back, then, is a register with names corresponding to the numbers, giving this picture —now in the author's personal collection—a permanent historical value.

The consequences of this brilliant victory

were, however, purely of a moral nature—the sins of the fathers were visited upon the sons.

As was to be expected, Edwin's wounds festered, and he had great difficulty in providing his worried mother with a believable story as to their origin. He was much astonished, moreover, that one night as he lay in a fever, an unknown hand tossed a large bouquet of lilacs through his window. For a long time he kept them in his clothes closet for fear of his mother's probing questions. Frau Quiebus herself was often terrorized during these disquieting times by appearances of ghosts. My most recent research, however, has shown that doubtless what lay behind these hauntings was the quick-change artistry of little Jadup, though it is probable that Lilith was the actual instigator. Let us linger yet a while with her.

Chapter Three

Short and sweet

No doubt of it, Lilith was wicked by nature; she was a devil. She dressed with enticing simplicity, preferring above all a cool sulphur-yellow. She had a silk scarf of that color with a long, wavy fringe, a present brought back to her from Venice by a disappointed lover. When she engaged in seduction, this scarf was her principle stage prop. Granted, women flirt just by being beautiful, but Frau Quiebus was quite wrong in claiming it was Lilith's fault that men fell for her simply because she looked at them. There is certainly nothing devilish about that, and in the beginning she was probably quite unaware of what she was doing. Later, however, she went about it out of pure, cunning cussedness—though in the name of a great and lofty ideal. By which I mean the house.

For Lilith adored her father, she truly idolized him. She was his servant. Of a morning she helped him pull on his boots, served him his coffee or wine, combed the crumbs out of his beard, aided him during the titanic onslaughts of her brothers. Powenz liked to have her light his cigarettes for him. He enjoyed having such a beautiful daughter. He called her his peach blossom, his gazelle. She was allowed to run massaging fingers through his hair when he was feeling blue and melancholy. "What a sweet little beast you are," he would then mumble.

I do not wish in any way to defend Lilith. By no means do I wish to gloss over her irresponsible actions. And yet I would ask that others not lend credence to every tale told about her, for some are told out of simple malice.

Nevertheless, in view of her commitment to the dream house, I consider it perfectly possible that she did indeed intentionally raise old man Knipfel's hopes, when, on the occasion of a charity bazaar and despite prevailing hostilities, he made bold, it is said, to approach her in a crudely clandestine manner. Armed, then, with a nosegay of violets, he appeared at a rendezvous beside the so-called Sour Spring in Kyps Woods, not once suspecting that Jadup, well concealed and with homemade camera in hand, was getting an irrefutable photographic record of various phases of the event.

The first shot clearly showed Knipfel playfully presenting the nosegay, which to keep fresh he had placed on his bald head under his hat. One can read Lilith's rejection from her pose, both in this picture and in the next, where, as she resists

The Powenz Ancestors

Upper left: Sir Pohwentz; upper right: Hokus Powenz;
lower left: Powo Powenz; lower right: Quirin Powenz

the old man's kisses, her disgust is plain to see. The scene of her slapping him was captured particularly well—Lilith aflame with virtue, Knipfel looking unutterably foolish. The last snapshot shows Lilith weeping bitterly, her blouse slightly open, her hair mussed, while a terribly disconcerted Knipfel remonstrates with her. They are surrounded by sun-drenched woods and blooming daisies.

The pictures were sharp and clear, and Knipfel had a very unpleasant shock when he received prints of them.

And although he gradually came to see through this shameless practical joke of which he was the butt, the part Knipfel had played was still a miserable one; moreover, he was a very married man. What else could he do but hold his peace and remit wicked Lilith a substantial sum out of his secret "amusement" fund, as "an expression of lasting affection"—and perhaps of some lasting hopes as well—and for her to buy "a little something" for herself.

"For the house," Lilith simply said as she handed the tidy sum to her father. Baltus accepted it with a smile.

"Productive revenge" was what her admiring brothers called their sister's successful campaign against Knipfel.

Chapter Four

Concerns heredity and mutation

To prevent their energies from being dispersed and wasted in individual actions, Baltus Powenz called a special sitting of the family council. Since it was a lovely, hot day, they met on Powenz Island, where he still managed the beach in summer. There beneath a mighty willow tree, amidst the warm scent of nettles and peppermint, the momentous council met without disturbance, for apart from them no one in Moessel ever went swimming before the first of July. As a precaution, however, they took up the planks of the narrow footbridge that joined the island to the mainland.

Even Heinrich had come along, though he suffered dreadfully from the gnats and flies, particularly from the variety of horsefly that emits no warning sound. He drew them all to him from great distances; they approached in concentric rings to suck his blood, every midge and mosquito, especially the one with the diabolical name of *anopheles*, the carrier of malaria. With a melancholy look on his face, Heinrich would constantly wave at them with a stick and try to chase them off without killing them. The obtrusive beasts simply loved his sweet blood. When the strain of having to listen to the humming at his ear finally led him to slap at himself, he would be quite depressed if he killed a mosquito in the process and would reproach himself bitterly.

The boys sat naked in a semicircle around their father Baltus. They were all molting painfully following the summer's first sunburn. Powenz arose, dark and thundering.

"O ye wretched fruits of these loins," he began and like a doomsaying prophet shook both fists at the town lying clearly visible and bathed in cheerful sunlight behind the gently rolling fields of wildflowers. "They have dealt foully with your father." (Hear, hear!) "You know that. They have let it be known that his presence is not wanted here in this lovely little corner of the earth. And I say fie upon a town that so despises the poorest and most devoted of its citizens, that begrudges us the very water for our coffee!" (Loud voice: If they even allowed us that!) "I say fie and double fie upon them." (The boys lifted their voices in chorus and Fabian added yet another muted "Fie!"). "But I appeal to you: that you, like me, will not rest until the insult done us is thoroughly avenged. O but think, ye incarnate tokens of a love that, though it at times be coarse is always sincere, do but think of

122

how you are the progeny of an illustrious family, that on your mother's side Corsican blood courses through your veins, do but think of that romantic figure, Giovanni of Ajaccio, a shabby urchin but a cousin to Bonaparte, who toward the end of the eighteenth century showed the beauty of his island to a young German merchant, who clung ardently to that gentleman when he once again put out to sea in his three-masted schooner, the *Giulio Cesare,* and who leapt into the sea with a cry of anguish, swimming after the ship, oblivious of death. The merchant, however, spied him and was so touched by such loyalty, by such a yearning for a new and happier life, that he had the youth, who was close to drowning, hauled on board, bringing him back to Germany with him and adopting him.

"Recall as well Hocus Powenz, your great-great-grandfather, the famous magician and illusionist, whose breast was adorned with medals bestowed upon him by all the potentates of Europe. Recall, too, his brother Monsieur Jacques Povence, the daredevil tightrope-walker and acrobat, or my own grandfather, an immortal clown who took his own life. Recall, moreover, if you will, that unpublished poet, that anonymous balladeer-harpist, Quirin Powenz, my very own father whom I add here not without emotion. For you must know that I am the firstborn of a poet.

"And do not forget Melchior Powenz, my fraternal blossom on the ever restless and roving family tree that bears our name, your dear uncle, who roamed this world first as a balloonist and parachute-artist, later as a bicycling vagabond, a royal tramp and wise man, an expert in love in all shades of yellow, black and brown, begetter of a mighty Powenzian clan from San Francisco to Dar es-Salaam, from Capetown to Spitsbergen. Nor forget my other brother, the unfortunate Hieronymus, who disappeared while in hot pursuit of mammon.

"Think of them all, here and now in this sunny and bee-buzzing hour of early summer, and let us follow the fearless, death-defying example of our forebears; and like these seemingly helpless water spiders here, let us walk upon the waves of existence, always playing, never sinking, undaunted by the gloom beneath us.

"In a somewhat bold turn of phrase, I described our family tree as ever restless and roving. But not I, Baltus Powenz, for I have grown weary of eternal wandering. I want to put down my roots here!"

Thus spoke Powenz, in no way a discredit to those ancestors he apostrophized—now with flaming tongue, now full of sentiment or righteous indignation. And his boys loudly slapped their naked thighs by way of applause.

This woke Fabian up. With a happy, dreamy smile he, too, belatedly joined in the applause.

They jumped up to take an oath, each with his arm extended to place his fingertip on the symbol of the house just above the spot where their father's heart was thudding dully.

All of which brings me to speak in greater detail about Jadup, and I do so with some reluctance, I must admit, because I am a bit doubtful whether by nature and general outlook on life I can be completely fair to this particular Powenz lad, whose cruelty, vanity and immorality are as well documented as is that strange charm he exerted on others from his earliest youth.

Even father Powenz, who normally found all babies hideous, is said to have remarked that Jadup looked like a little god. Of all the children, by the way, he was the only one that Sabina could not nurse—for which the lad never forgave her. Very early on, cigarettes constituted his principal source of nourishment.

Nature must be held responsible for having displayed such criminal affection for this child when it came to physical beauty. I use the word criminal because the invisible little god that dwelt within this charming temple of flesh and blood was so cruel, because his soul was so cruel. Even those who loved him admitted that he was a boy without heart, and if someday, as the old fairy tale has it, his heart should no longer beat in his own breast, but in that of a little bird, then it will be in that of an iridescent kingfisher.

Just as an example: Antonin, a passionate lad of the same age who lived upstairs in the same house, fell totally under Jadup's spell. Unbidden, he would follow him about—which was certainly not Jadup's fault.

For Jadup did not love him. He was a stranger to all affection; he was merely amused by the boy. But just for the nasty delight of his soul—hard and brittle as glass—he made good use of Antonin's slavish devotion.

Jadup said, "Here, friend of mine, take this rough pebble and put it in your shoe. Walk around like that for three days—and I don't want to see you make a single face the whole time." And Antonin did it without question. He did it as one would do it for a god, as if it would win him divine grace; he did it, not knowing that besides himself there were about a dozen other boys running around with equally painful pebbles in their shoes— smiling, never wincing or resting—all to please Jadup.

This is no place to go into particulars about the other abominable diversions to which this lad introduced his unlucky admirers, both big and little—some of them even *in cumulo*. And not, as one might think, as their friend, but as an animal-trainer with whip in hand. But one fact cannot be suppressed: it is almost unbelievable the way these infatuated lads were willing to bear every humiliation without a murmur (e.g., having to creep to school on all fours, or to swallow live earthworms, or to perform similar foul deeds), and there is simply no explaining the whys or wherefores.

There is one documented instance that fully reveals Jadup's heartlessness. One day when all the other Powenzes were not at home, he asked Antonin, who served him as a serf would, to come over at an appointed hour, knowing full well that he would arrive on the dot.

But as Antonin entered the room, he found Jadup unconscious on the floor, bathed in blood from a dagger plunged to the hilt into his heart. The horrified lad fled screaming for help. But when Antonin returned, there sat Jadup at the window; he smiled as if nothing had happened and asked in great astonishment whatever could be wrong with his friend, and why he was crying and pale as a ghost. Jadup had, of course, cleaned up every trace of his gruesome masquerade. And so Antonin was forced to conclude that he had been fooled by some feverish hallucination, for he swore his eyes had beheld his master lying dead and bathed in blood.

As a curious footnote, one ought to add that

127

not long afterwards poor Antonin met a fate very similar to the one Jadup had so cynically played out before him. And the last thing his mortal eyes saw as he bled to death was Jadup's impassive face above his own.

Possibly, as many people maintain, it was Jadup's voice that charmed everyone. He knew its magic power and used it to extract someone's most fragile secrets before he even knew what had happened. But in the end Eros punished him as well.

Jadup had a passion for getting himself up in costumes, and he especially loved to wander about as a ghost. He had the rare good fortune of once seeing a real, live mayor flee weeping and wailing at the sight of him.

I once came across him sitting on a stoop. He was weeping, and so bitterly, that it truly cut me to the heart. His eyes were bloodshot, he sobbed, his supple body was convulsed with the profoundest grief. Touched deeply, I sat down next to him in an expression of sympathy, hoping to comfort him and to learn the cause of such desperate sorrow, when suddenly he stuck his tongue out at me and took off with a loud, mocking laugh.

I am now almost fully convinced that he used this genius he had for imitating others to carry out all sorts of dastardly intrigues. Rumor has it that he took malicious and puerile pleasure in dressing up as a teenage girl in order to win the trust of a number of young ladies from very good homes in the neighboring town of Maarfurt, learning all the inmost thoughts and desires of their hearts.

At the council of war held on the beach, however, he revealed the depth of his sordid nature.

Now it is true that Kaspar gladly volunteered to punish their common enemy in his own way by striking at the most sensitive spot, that is, by offering to seduce Herr Gockeley's innocent daughter. But the cruelest and most effective proposal came from wicked little Jadup. He said:

"Behold yonder town lying so sanctimoniously in the sun. Father! Brothers! Call down a curse upon her! Call swarms of insects down upon her.[9] Let the heavens turn black with flies and rumble with the hum of bumblebee hordes. Train all bees from henceforth to sting only Quiebuses, Knipfels and Gockeleys! Let the wasps, those tigers of the insect world, wheel and dart, together with a cavalry of dreadful hornets. Call up the woodlice, earwigs and creepy centipedes; let caterpillars surge over our enemies' yards, eating the fruits of their gardens; enlist the cockroaches, always scurrying and always stinking, to invade the kitchens and pantries of our enemies. Above all, do not forget the household pests—the fleas, the bedbugs, the lice. Breed them, let them mul-

[9]Compare Goethe's *Faust*, Part II, Act II, Scene 1.

tiply until they become a great and terrible chastisement. Waahoo, I have spoken."

Father Powenz had followed the impassioned words of his son Jadup with growing enthusiasm, and now he took both his hands and shook them. His eyes were moist.

"You have our thanks, dear son," Powenz said, looking off to one side to conceal his emotion.

Chapter Five

Shake well before using

The days that followed are part of Moessel's history now, but those who lived through them still feel the itch.

With a doggedness and precision that was peculiarly their own, the Powenz family began to raise up a great plague over Moessel. People suspected who was behind it all, but could not catch them at it.

By its very nature, the enterprise demanded the most careful preparation. And here, once again, Fabian sacrificed his precious sleep for the good of the family, as he put it. He was already so fat that his bed had had to be widened. His invention of the long-loaf, moreover, enabled him to consume his breakfast all in one fell swoop. (He was too lazy to cut open and butter one hard roll after the other.) Fabian said:

"Heinrich, gentle brother of mine, can you tell me the method, rate and yield of reproduction for the following creatures: a) fleas b) bedbugs c) lice—and of the latter 1) head, and 2) body?"

Heinrich answered: "O terrible Fabian, what are you planning to do? The flea is the noblest of the three. To my knowledge, it lays but twelve eggs. Six days later these become slender white larva, which pupate after eleven days, and only then, after yet another eleven days, does the pupa become a flea."

Fabian said, "Fine, and b)?"

Once again Heinrich answered, "The bedbug bears young four times a year; ah, but the louse brings forth five thousand offspring in eight weeks, each of them sexually mature within eighteen days and..."

The brothers decided to begin at once to breed the species with the most obvious chances of success. Uncle Melchior, the famous vagabond, who happened to be rolling through Moessel, was quite prepared to provide the necessary breeding stock in the form of tom-fleas, he-lice and bedbugesses, for he knew all sorts of tramps and beggars, who for a small fee could deliver promptly and bountifully. Only Heinrich at first refused to participate, but, good soul that he was, he promised at least to breed some of his grasshoppers, caterpillars and snails en masse and to set them out into enemy gardens.

The master plan called for a massive one-time infestation of the most insolent of their adversaries, meaning the Knipfel, Gockeley, Quiebus and

Jadup Powenz

Dattel households, plus those of about a dozen other worthy personages.

"Filial love and loyalty," Powenz would cry with emotion each time he visited the breeding station.

Agile Jadup had charge of the fleas and Zephirin of the bedbugs, but Violand had the lice. The critters thrived splendidly indeed under such constant care, while the boys had great fun tending them. At the end, in fact, they parted most unwillingly with their little charges. It had proved something of a humanistic education for them all.

The difficult question was how to put the creatures to effective use without being discovered.

The enemy houses were kept under strict surveillance for several weeks in order to seize at once any opportunity to smuggle in the little parasites and bloodsuckers. Featherbeds and carpets spread for airing were used successfully for the purpose. Whenever the family was out and the windows were open, slingshots volleyed in little flea-pills, wads of gauze wrapped around a stone and an insect, which later freed itself when once inside. Or the little helpmeets were let loose at the front door—especially bedbugs, who dislike light and who were herded and maneuvered through the cracks in the door by flashlight. Mice also served as couriers.

The effects were not long in coming—in part

because as soon as the dreadful discovery was made, the horrified housewives only too gladly kept the shameful fact secret, but principally because it was usually a rather long time before the state of emergency was recognized for what it was. And by then it was already too late.

It was at a soirée at Frau Quiebus's that the infestation was first noticeably felt. The consequences were dreadful. Almost every guest suffered unutterably, but dared not speak out. A wave of agonized rubbings and scratchings, concealed only with great effort, swept through the formally-dressed assemblage, and the young ladies smiled stony smiles of secret torment. In desperation the gentlemen smoked cigars and blew the smoke up their sleeves; they rubbed themselves surreptitiously against the wall or on the edges of chairs as they passed by. At first no one suspected that everyone else was suffering just as much as he. Soon, however, it was common knowledge in town that one got—can you believe it?—fleas in Frau Quiebus's house, where they apparently multiplied at an incredible rate in the nap of her costly persian carpets.

Suddenly both Edwin and Carola showed signs of great discomfort and exhibited suspicious red spots all over their bodies, especially in the softer portions, spots which Frau Quiebus tearfully recognized as the measles. She sent her son and daughter to bed at once and sent urgently for Doctor Flaum, who, after he had given a detailed report of his own ailments in a voice almost devoid of all hope, said that the spots were in all likelihood none other than the bites of the so-called body louse, a most troublesome and, what was more, in no way harmless parasite, since, as was well known, it was the specific carrier of typhoid fever. Doctor Flaum was, by the way, one of the few citizens of Moessel who looked favorably on the Powenzes. In his opinion, a little bit of healthy Powenzialism never hurt anyone.

Doctor Flaum came twice daily, conscientiously took the pulse and temperature of the lice-infested children, and with a mournful air instituted the necessary measures for delousing the infested household. Among other things, he recommended as especially effective a certain insect powder that was constantly praised in the Moesseler classified ads and was manufactured by a local firm, the name of which was innocuous enough, but whose real owner was Baltus Powenz. The preparation was in great demand. At Jadup's suggestion, it had been mixed with itching powder and was accompanied by detailed directions for its use, cast in verse form by Violand, crudely illustrated by Zephirin and bearing the general title, "The Perfect Exterminator."[10]

[10]Out of print.

136

Following this embarrassing discovery, Frau Quiebus immediately dismissed her housemaids, clearly an act of injustice. They certainly had not been the intended target of the Powenz attack, but the hapless employees had now become innocent civilian casualties of these insidious battle tactics. It is also true that, contrary to what might be expected, the heartless Powenzes never made use of third parties. They always did things on their own.

The poor housemaids, then, were struck down as well. But though their dismissal was unjust as far as the plague of fleas and lice was concerned, it is no secret that for years Rosa the cook had fattened her bankbook with considerable sums by juggling the kitchen accounts for a penny here, a penny there, all at the cost of Frau Quiebus; while Fanny the parlormaid had long been secretly looking for a better job and would shortly have given notice anyway "to go take care of her sick mother."

Thus to the initiate are revealed those hidden links between true and false innocence, between just and unjust punishment, and things that seem to be without causality are shown to obey a higher, more serene order.

Frau Quiebus did not regard these dismissals as unwelcome events, for ever since Edwin had arrived at puberty, she had decided on principle to hire only especially ugly housemaids, whom she nevertheless constantly assumed were possible compromisers of the lad's innocence. She was of the strange belief that these girls might suddenly throw themselves on Edwin's bed, which was the reason for her constant urgings that he always keep the door to his room closed and barred.

All of Moessel itched and scratched, and one consequence of the plague was that the victims, being the highly respected families that they were, suspected perfectly innocent acquaintances of having introduced this curse of Satan into their homes.

Overnight guests were suspected of a lack of personal hygiene and were astonished to find that they were not invited back. Wedding engagements declined. The schools were also held responsible—maybe the children had brought the beasts home with them. A printed flyer appeared, bearing excellent—and malicious—caricatures. The regional press made witty comments. The whole thing was quite embarrassing for the good town of Moessel.

At the instigation of Frau Quiebus, the police went around to have a look at the Powenz apartment on the flimsy pretext of being interested in sanitation, but actually in hopes of discovering the center of infestation. But thanks to a first-class intelligence service, the pack was fully prepared to meet this committee of inquiry. Exemplary order reigned; everything sparkled with cleanliness. They had certainly gone to a great deal of trouble. On the wall hung a hygiene calendar, a wooden tablet with the classical maxim *Mens sana in corpore sano* burnt into it, and an informational chart put out by the health department, on which the insects in question were pictured with disgusting realism and magnified a hundred times over. And though the district physician for Moessel used his magnifying glass to examine all cracks and crevices (and the necks and wrists of all the boys as well), he was unable to find the least bit of evidence. The incubators, of course, had long since been put to the torch.

When the investigation was over, father Powenz made a straightforward request for a certificate declaring that the health department had found his home to be a humble one perhaps, but impeccable in matters of hygiene. The bewildered doctor quite simply could not refuse him. No one in Moessel, not even the mayor at that point, could boast such an official declaration of cleanliness. All this took place in June, 1914—that is, shortly before the Great War.

Chapter Six

*Which discusses certain disruptions caused by
an act of God and how the Powenz pack dealt
with them—Together with a
dionysiac intermezzo*

It is no wonder that when war broke out, the general expectation in Moessel was that this godless and unpatriotic pack would now show its true, i.e., vile colors. Frau Quiebus, for one, stated publicly that she would not be at all surprised if such suspicious characters were unmasked as enemy spies and every last one of them shot as a common traitor. Most certainly these wild, unruly fellows would refuse to serve in the army—or they would desert or mutiny. In these times of pure and selfless patriotism, the Powenzes could not long endure, most assuredly not—that, at least, was what everyone said. Presumably one of them would chop off an index finger or shoot himself in the foot, as was sometimes done even in peacetime when a young man wanted to shirk his military duty; most certainly they would smoke cigarettes to such excess that their hearts would be weakened.

Nothing of the sort happened.

Just the opposite. In all of Moessel there was hardly another family that greeted the outbreak of war with such honest enthusiasm as the Powenzes did.

Kaspar, the eldest, was immediately called up, since he was in the reserves. But that was a stroke of good fortune, for he could walk right into the butcher's or baker's and shop for whatever he pleased. Those good merchants did not want to refuse him outright, despite the rather large amounts owed them; they could not deny him his hard rolls or juicy sirloin when he stood there in the king's uniform ready to defend his country in war, when he might well be dead before the week was out. They shook his hand, and he shook heartily back without a second thought. But Sabina, his mother, wept.

Scarcely was the news out that Kaspar Powenz would be joining up, when all the girls and ladies, all his loves past and present, started prettying themselves up, for each hoped to see him just once more.

Jadup, who knew every one of them on sight, watched with great interest as with infinite slowness they all walked past the Elephant House to no apparent purpose but the chance of meeting Kaspar. Jadup recognized Jorkum's young wife, who gazed at the tobacco shop window for hours on end, until friends of hers happened along. Then with a blush, she sauntered on up the street, only to turn right back again as if remembering something she had forgotten and then waited patiently for hours on end, staring at the dreary display in the bike-shop window. They all passed by, casting inconspicuous glances at the Powenz's windows. Hermine came by, and Babette, and even Frau von Uhlenkamp and Abigail; and each brought along something that she wanted to give him—cigarettes, a ring, a magic stone, an amulet to protect him against being killed or wounded.

But Kaspar came home very late that night, for he had been saying his goodbyes to Renate and Regina, the twins who loved him with all their hearts, loved him in perfect harmony and with no jealousy whatever.

But somehow, one after the other, Kaspar met with them all and took his farewell; from the inconsolable Frau Jorkum in an entryway, from Elsa Kapf, the proctor's daughter, in Moessel Academic's physics lab, which just happened to be empty. There among all the shiny glass and metal they were undisturbed. He arranged to meet Abigail in the woods in the evening and helped ardent Frau von Uhlenkamp climb through his window late at night. His brothers very tactfully pretended to be asleep.

And Kaspar simply had to love them all—one for her generous mouth, another for her hair, still another for the fragrance of her body or for her neck or breasts. And so each in her way loosed the magic spell of his desire.

And as toward morning he walked to the train station (for his regiment was quartered elsewhere), his lady friends all stood amicably beside one another, waving. It really was a very pretty sight. For each in her own way was especially lovely.

When the train finally pulled out, mighty Kaspar saw many of them weeping, embracing and gazing devotedly in each other's eyes, sisters sharing a common fate.

Only the twins waited for the train by a crossing outside of town. What a strange sight they were; there was something eerie about the way they looked so much alike. There they stood on the embankment, one creature twice over, and waved as their friend passed by.

The Powenzes were not lazy by nature, even if they were not exactly capable of taking on regular, honest work. But now that the war was on, an exceptional circumstance in itself, they truly came to life for the first time. "Doctor" Powenz—the title stuck, no matter what—set about to convert his factory. This was indeed not the time for all his (and his boys') favorite inventions and wares for the practical-joke market—the itching powders, the deceptive replicas of little piles of dog dirt, the black enameled tin cutouts that looked for all the world like spilled ink. For all these and other merry bits of mischief it was now decidedly not the time.

And so the whole family worked with glowing zeal at producing red, white and black flags. Their countless variations on patriotic knickknacks sold well and were soon distributed throughout Germany.

There were, for example, spittoons with a picture of Poincaré inside, wrought-iron bootjacks in the form of a Russian with both arms raised in surrender, handkerchiefs with the portrait of the kaiser or of various famous generals, inkwells shaped like grenades, ditto schnapps bottles, and so on.

They were making money as never before, but then, of course, they needed it. They loyally continued to pool all earnings in the family kitty, which is not to say that each might not secretly hold back smaller amounts on special occasions. Violand, for instance, carried on a quite profitable trade in magic bullets and protective talismans to be hung around the neck.

And because the Powenzes succeeded in meeting the massive surge in demand for patriotic fancy goods by having a sharp sense for what was wanted and by providing a ready supply of it, and because business really was good, they had no reason whatever for finding fault with the grim god of war.

Here let me make mention of one small occurrence. On the evening of that memorable day on which war was declared, Doctor Powenz had gone to Adam's Wineshop to drink a little something, just as he had done on the day of his arrival in Moessel. And in honor of the war and in consequence of a great many other toasts as well, especially to the health of the imperial family, he found he had drunk so much that he could not negotiate the way home all on his own. So he sat there and did not budge, singing "Deutschland über alles" with a thick tongue.

Smiling and babbling, there he sat, massive and immovable, like some drunken heathen deity with indestructible hempen hair and beard, large hands and broad, florid face. Herr Adam, the innkeeper, however, was a small and timid man who did not dare approach his guest, well aware of how terrible was that rage when aroused.

But on this first evening of the war—as so often before—Frau Powenz sent out her full complement of sons to bring their father home. They found him enjoying a little nap.

The three older boys, Kaspar, Fabian and Heinrich, emptied their father's glass for him and then lifted him up. Zephirin bore the mighty head in both hands to prevent it from hanging down, and Violand walked on ahead, carrying a magnesium torch he had cleverly remembered to bring

145

along to give the homeward procession a festive air. Jadup, the youngest, brought up the rear, piping warlike melodies on his harmonica. Thus they bore their dear father home and brought him safely to his bed.

That very night, however, in his inebriated state and with a great, loud cry, he sired a son, Jubal—which means joy.

The Powenzes had a sure instinct, devoid of all sentimentality, for making good commercial use of the war; but that did not remain their sole activity during this period.

They alone were behind many of the rumors that began to surface at the time; but fortunately for them, they were never discovered. They had great fun spreading them, though: Germany was just crawling with spies whose immediate, nefarious mission was to poison all water supplies. And naturally they were highly gratified to hear that the moment she heard the news, Frau Quiebus swore to abstain from water in any form whatsoever. She was afraid even to wash herself. The Powenzes were, of course, the ones who had all the latest information about the shipment of money that was said to be in transit across Germany on its way from France to Russia, in a black car that traveled soundlessly and without lights, and who knew but what it might very well pass through those towns where it was least expected—through Moessel, for instance.

146

The news had its effect. Under the leadership of Herr Knust, those patriots too old for military service banded together with but one burning desire—to capture those enemy billions. They guarded the highways, dug them up, barricaded them with other cars, and within a very short time caused extensive damage; they brought traffic to a standstill and shot at harmless pedestrians —until finally the nonsense was forbidden by military order.

The sad thing was—so went another rumor that cropped up right away—that no sooner had the watch been lifted, than the car with the money drove right down the main street of Moesel and was now, of course, well over the Russian border.

A large, robust lady with somewhat hard features, Fraulein Schlagintweit by name, who came from Bremen, was selected by the ever-inventive Violand Powenz as the victim of a successful prank. In those excitable days, just one word sufficed for anyone to be immediately suspected of being a spy. And it really seemed quite plausible that Fraulein Schlagintweit was a man dressed as a woman. Egged on by Violand, a swarm of screaming schoolboys at once began following the innocent young lady down the street. Soon adults, too, were making menacing gestures at her.

As a result, the young lady walked faster and faster—and that really was suspicious. She protested her innocence with a Bremen twang, which was at once recognized as broken German with a strong foreign accent. She was then seized—roughly, since she was a man—and handed over to the police. Only after hard-nosed Police Sergeant Kolb had assured the waiting mob that the lady was not a man and in no way a suspicious character, did the crowd disperse—not in the least embarrassed either, merely dissatisfied and grumbling. The Powenz pack laughed.

Chapter Seven

In praise of Violand

With seven children of the Powenz sort and in a family in such glorious disarray as this one, it can easily happen that no one notices right off if one of them is missing. And since, moreover, no Powenz ever ratted on another if he happened to stay out all night raising hell or making love, it should come as no surprise that several days passed before it was discovered that Violand was gone.

Without a word of goodbye, the scamp had left home. And did not come back till weeks later.

Following his disappearance, it was at first assumed that he had tried to volunteer for the army, even though he was only sixteen.

He was a rangy young fellow with a dry skin that tanned quickly. He never sweated. And he had one distinguishing mark—not that he was truly cross-eyed, but his left eye wandered some-times, perhaps as the result of a weak muscle. It obeyed the more lively, agile glance of the other only very slowly; it was always just a bit too late, which lent it a melancholy look. And while the one was a pronounced blue, the sad one was closer to brown. This trick of nature gave Violand his special, almost mysterious charm. In general, he was the neatest of the brothers. He tended somewhat to delusions of grandeur. In a restaurant he would have the page address him as "My lord" and call him to the telephone—"My lord, a long-distance call from Berlin!" He loved to dispatch telegrams from the train, much to the astonishment of his fellow passengers. It should be added that, to the last man, the Powenzes left Moessel only very unwillingly.

When Violand returned home, he was wearing a field-gray infantry uniform; but it was much too large, so that there was something both touching and warlike about him. In his lapel he wore the black and white ribbon of the Iron Cross. Apparently he had been wounded, too, for at his brow was a bandage that was always bloodstained.

What a joy for every patriot, to watch the way he would walk through Moessel at a leisurely pace and with the dashing poise of the seasoned front-line soldier, to see the way he saluted, so stiff and smart with a minimum of effort. Stout Herr Knust put down the brush with which he was painting his flagpole to shake the hand of this young warrior and say, "God bless you and all heroes, my lad!"

At home he was greeted with a loud "halloo!"

"Oh, you little whippersnapper!" said old Powenz as he raised a threatening finger. "But you've hit the bull's-eye."

He studied him as would an expert savoring an especially successful disguise; he fingered the material and praised the miscellany of buttons that gave the uniform its look of genuine wear and tear.

Violand's story was that after he had slipped away from home, a deed for which he now begged forgiveness, he had smuggled himself up to the war zone as a kind of stowaway in a troop transport. A good-natured sergeant, a tough old veteran who was touched by the bravery of the boy, had watched out for him. And when he had begged and pleaded for heaven's sake not to be sent back home, the sarge had grinned and put the ecstatic lad in a uniform. Because he was such a plucky kid, those rough soldiers had pampered him, and he was soon the mascot of the regiment.

It appeared that in the course of one ill-fated skirmish (Violand's military word), he had distinguished himself quite famously. He described it only very sketchily and with some reluctance, intentionally detracting from his own role. The commander of his regiment, so the tale went, had been wounded by a direct hit in the chest, and Violand had hacked his way through a dozen of the enemy, black and white Frenchmen, to save him from being taken prisoner; he had defended the commander at the risk of his own life and brought him safely back. Soon thereafter, unfortunately, he had himself been wounded by a piece of shrapnel—nothing serious, but painful nevertheless. And he was able to show everyone the stupid, jagged piece of iron that the corps surgeon had removed, to which there still clung, unmistakable and ghastly, bits of congealed blood and hair. And now he would have to hang around until the scratch healed—that is, just for a few days—while out there there was work to be done, which did not please him at all.

The story appeared in all the papers. Moessel now gladly forgave its hero every prank and paid him well for that ominous bit of shrapnel so visibly stained with hero's blood. In fact, he sold several dozen pieces in no time, always with the request that the buyer not tell anyone, since it had actually been promised to someone else.

With each trophy of war that he so casually let himself be talked out of, there was a little wild and woolly tale he could tell; and precisely because personal memories were attached to it, he did not let it go—as anyone could understand—very willingly and then only at considerable recompense, for these were, after all, spoils taken at the risk of life and limb—French caps, cockades, copper pull

Violand Powenz

rings from hand grenades, dud shells still in one piece, case shot, or even pilot's insignia, all picked up cheaply from his real comrades in arms. He had his own secret price list.

So-called lifesavers were in particular demand. These were dented cigarette cases that had just managed to ward off the fatal shot, or watches with shrapnel still implanted in them, or letters from a sweetheart that by some magic spell had broken the bullet's force.

Violand could not come up with enough of these curios; but he also knew how to manufacture them to look like the genuine article—in which task Jadup gladly assisted him.

Of course, there was not one ounce of truth to the shameless fellow's story—Violand had never really been at the front. Even father Powenz, who saw through him right off, had raised a finger in warning. Violand had, to be sure, tried to volunteer, although mainly out of curiosity. And wherever he had gone, he had been well taken care of, but had always been turned down because of his youth. And so he had knocked around from one garrison to another, until he had learned enough about barracks life to manage on his own. He let his head wound heal rapidly by having the bandage grow smaller and smaller; and then dashing Violand once again "returned to the front."

He had in time become bored with the tedious

merchandizing of war trophies. And so, dressed as a lieutenant and with his wounded arm in a sling and the Iron Cross, First class, on his breast, he went out on a tour of "dumb little" country towns—and did very well.

"I am really being spoiled more than I deserve," he wrote home modestly.

> "At the moment I am in charge of military training for a group of boys and am having a roaring good time doing it.
>
> "The lads are really splendid and think the world of me. Our war games are both admired and feared by the populace in the neighboring villages. People assure me that a nation with officers like me is undefeatable. I have been seriously considering having papa come for an inspection tour I could arrange for him. Naturally he would have to come dressed as a general, which would cause great delight here. Yesterday at a victory celebration that I organized, I gave a fine patriotic speech. And I am welcome in the best homes."

To tell the truth, Violand was quite successful in his job as a trainer of patriotic youth, and he received voluntary contributions for his efforts. And it was not long before an old general, a real one, came for a perfectly serious inspection of the troops, dispensing high praise both for the boys' superb discipline and élan as well as for their valiant leader.

Violand got along so famously in the military that it was all the same whether he was really an officer or whether his impersonation was so good that he was taken for one wherever he went.

In the third year of the war, I met him at the front near Ferme Trouchy, for in the meantime he had become a real soldier, without his escapade's having ever been found out. By now he had truly earned his Iron Cross, had indeed bravely rescued his CO and shortly afterwards received a severe head wound. I saw the poor devil as he lay there. With a slow, despairing gesture he reached up to his bulging forehead, only to give a quick flick of his hand as if he wanted to shake off some unappetizing stuff that had stuck to his fingers. And then his half-paralyzed mouth smiled an indescribable smile. But miraculously, he did recover, although he was a mute for the rest of his life and lost all sense of smell.

Chapter Eight

*Should be regarded as the introduction
to the next chapter*

There was something truly prophetic about
Violand's hijinks in those first few weeks of war.
But he was not the only one with a talent for
making the dull events of life's diurnal course
more appealing, for putting a pretty face on existence and trying to alter the ways of providence a
bit with a few cheering embellishments.

It had long been the boys' custom, when of an
evening they sat in bed for a while having a smoke,
to tell one another stories about what all had happened to them that day. They would marvel at
Kaspar, the expert in matters of love, and would
take delight in Violand's gleeful talent for lying
and Jadup's amusing ghost stories. Even Heinrich's peculiar observations were heard with sympathy and much shaking of heads. He had the
habit of taking his camera to bed with him—for
the longest time now, he had wanted to get some
snapshots of his dreams. It just had to be possible,
he maintained stubbornly; all you had to do was
catch the right moment, sort of in the middle of

things between being not quite asleep and not really quite awake anymore either. He imagined how wonderful it would be. No one had ever tried it before. But every morning he had to admit, "I just can't seem to catch it right, and..." His brothers' indelicate term for him was "poor screwball."

Fabian, the next to the oldest, would normally have fallen asleep by then, since there was nothing he loved so much in life as sleep. Not that when he was asleep he was fully inactive. He was a regular dream artist—meaning that he was blessed with the unusual talent of not losing the awareness that he was dreaming while he slept. Thus he could take the events of his dreams, and if he did not like what was going on, he would give them whatever twist for the better he pleased. If, for example, a lion would attack him in a dream and devour him, he was perfectly capable of splitting himself in two right at the last moment, becoming both Fabian and the ferocious lion. Grunting with pleasure, he would relish the taste of dining on himself, all the while enjoying that very special, creepy feeling of being eaten alive. Afterwards, he would claim, licking his chops, that he had tasted very good, something like roast goose stuffed with apples. Jadup confessed that he never had such good dreams, and gentle Heinrich asked in alarm if the lion had hurt him much.

And he made love almost exclusively in his

dreams; Fabian loved, but in his sleep. When he was awake he was simply too lazy. He was inordinately fat and always cheerfully drowsy. And though he was very inventive when it came to recipes and melodies (the latter hummed in his sleep), his most useful talents were doubtless in mathematics. Father Powenz gladly consulted him about the plans for the house.

Fabian's laziness was downright incredible. It alone explains why he so seldom fell in love.

"Oh my," he groaned, "I'm supposed to go over and see Johanna. She's such a cheerful, grateful girl. Ah, Kaspar, or how about you, Heinrich, couldn't one of you take over love's labor for me?"

And he readily promised them a nice present, or even money, if they would be so good as to do the job for him. He himself preferred to sleep.

I have heard tell that once over Easter vacation, a rainy one, admittedly, Fabian Powenz slept right on through from the first day to the last, a period of fourteen days, making allowance for when he stopped to eat. That had been, he confessed with a yawn, his most pleasant vacation ever. It took the united efforts of his brothers to wake him. It was useless to shout at him or shoot off a pistol near his ear or tickle his nose with a straw. At best he would give a funny little sneeze or purr softly, but he would never wake up. And water poured from a watering can was simply greeted with the motions of a swimmer. But thanks to a clever gadget, his bed could be tipped over like a dump truck, tossing him onto the floor. Even then, he would snuggle up in his blanket and go right on sleeping. If he slowly began to come to himself at last, a state he called "dozy dawn," he would scold his brothers as heartless fellows who held nothing sacred and showed no reverence for that most precious of nature's gifts, sweet sleep.

But now the blithely lazy Fabian—to whom mankind is indebted for that most blessed of inventions, the musical coffee mill—was especially and desperately needed for thinking up new wartime knickknacks. He would lie cozily in bed, talking in his sleep, as it were.

"How would it be," he might say for instance, "if we manufactured miniature soldiers' graves, make them out of plaster with tiny gravestones. You could design them so that there would be a little glass picture frame for a snapshot of the dear departed. The whole thing could be put on the bedroom dresser. My guess is it would sell well. Or maybe you could run off lithographs, in lots of bright colors, showing the battlefield at sunset, with signal flares exploding and troops hurrahing, while in their midst the kaiser personally pins an Iron Cross on a soldier's breast. But leave the face of the soldier blank on purpose, so that a family could fill it in with a picture of their loved one."

Whatever Fabian suggested along these lines, did well; the items sold. He had an infallible nose for kitsch.

For all their attention to foreign enemies, the Powenzes never forgot their domestic ones. They remained irreconcilable, despite the fact that those patriotic days saw the hearts of the Moesselers disposed to greater charity. Many an old feud was buried; even Frau Quiebus, who did not easily forgive and forget, brought herself to work in the Red Cross side by side with the wife of Professor Hornpostler, who as a former waitress had till then been justifiably excluded from the best Moessel society. (This state of affairs was, however, set to rights once again as soon as the war came to its unhappy conclusion.)

To be sure, the tempo of battle between the Powenz clan and their enemies slackened considerably during the war. But there were little scrimmages, just so that no one forgot that there was to be no sniveling sentimentality in the matter.

Kaspar Powenz, now a noncommissioned officer, had badly wounded a hand when a homemade grenade had exploded, and he was home on leave for a while. He had the great pleasure of giving basic training to Emil Knipfel, the somewhat dreamy-eyed son of the town surveyor. He was very thorough. Poor Knipfel was given those well-loved orders, "On the ground! On your feet!"

so often—to the obvious amusement of the youth of Moessel who sat watching from the drill field fence—that in the end he could do it better than any other soldier in the whole German army. This practical exercise was to save his life on the battlefield many a time.

Besides Kaspar, Heinrich also served in the military.

It is only natural, however, that such a gentle lad went to war not as a bearer of arms but as a medic. He belonged to those hybrid creatures who were more the menials of war than its soldiers and who were ostensibly safe from bodily harm. But on closer inspection, medics proved to be largely the sort of people who had not left home all in one piece. One fellow was missing a finger, another was handicapped, while still another stuttered. Many of them had been employed in steambaths or beauty shops—in trades, that is, with something feminine about them. Writers were also found in their ranks.

Heinrich had always regarded his own appearance with very great aversion. And he really was not handsome, what with his astonished, freckled face, his mahogany cow-eyes and his large, beet-red ears. He took it for granted that no one could possible love him, and he was always surprised when someone was nice to him. Tradition has passed on something he once said that reflects just how much of a loner he was: "I could never like anyone who loved someone like me," he is reported to have said. "And naturally I don't appeal to the people I like. I don't even know what love is good for, though I've heard its praises sung on occasion."

Nevertheless he found some fine comrades-in-arms. But very soon his first pal got shot in the stomach (and he played and played his harmonica half the night, then laid it aside and was dead). His second friend came from Hanover, and they had the best talks about plants and animals; but he was gassed and went insane. The third comrade—and Heinrich liked him the best—was a jolly fellow from Jueterbog; a grenade tore him to bits before Heinrich's eyes. The head landed in Heinrich's lap, and lifting it up by the hair, he asked, "Will we ever be able to laugh again or love and... Oh, Karl," he continued talking to the head, "your face is still warm and your eyes and mouth still moist. Just now you were looking right at me, you laughed, you were alive, and now you're dead and...."

Incredulous, he placed the head with the body and thought, "That's the way he was before." And still he could not believe it. But then when he was all alone with the dead man, whose steaming, warm blood had dyed his lap red, he screamed to him: "Comrade, arise and walk!"

But there was no God to help him.

I myself once saw a lance corporal from the Bohemian Forest, whose arm had been ripped off by shrapnel (though lucky for him the stump was dressed and bound right away), pack the dead limb in a sandbag and have it brought with him to the field hospital because he was absolutely sure that the staff surgeon could sew it back on again. He just shook his head when he found out it was not the case.

"Now that's stupid. That's really what I'd call stupid, that you can't do that much," he said scornfully to the doctor.

Heinrich did not eat meat, and so he often went hungry. He did not eat it because he did not have the heart to let some great, fine beast like a cow be slaughtered just to nourish him. Likewise, he did not pick flowers and could not stand to see a lawn mowed—it cut him to the quick. For he had a profound reverence for all living things. But they all called him "sterile Heinrich," and that always made him terribly angry.

He would shudder whenever the staff doctor used his fingernail to scratch at a scab during sick call; or when there was a general medical inspection, he would blush at the sight of such a phalanx of virile nakedness.

Even fat Fabian had had to follow the colors. But he was the envy of his comrades for his ability to fall into a refreshing sleep without further ado the moment he was off duty—whether sitting or lying, whatever the weather, impervious to all noise, even exploding grenades. And when he was once asleep, the gods granted him his every earthly desire without his ever having to lift a finger.

It is well known how once, when fire broke out in the three old sisters' apartment upstairs—directly over his head—he calmly stayed in bed. All he did was ask Jadup to reach up and feel if the ceiling was hot yet.

No one understood army talk as well as the Powenzes; no one knew the ways of the trenches as well as they. For fellows like them, war was a glorious carnival; they thought nothing of it, for by nature they were brave and fearless. That the war was "a pain" was Fabian's constant comment, and every Powenz, including Heinrich, called it a hoax. But all they meant was that despite its tragic aspects, the war merely seemed to be going on, that it was an illusion, a distortion of something else, of men playing soldiers, perhaps. It was enough, they told themselves, to pretend there was a war on; and, what with the brothers' theatrical talents plus their natural good looks and perfect contempt for death, why, they simply came to full, natural bloom out on the battlefield.

We already know how, with just the merest gesture, Violand could look the picture of total discipline, meeting every military requirement from "At ease!" to "Attention!" with a minimum of expended energy. And if you watched very closely, you saw nothing more than a twitch, a charge of electric current, a keen look in the eyes, a reflex of the cheeks. The way Violand knew how to say "Yes, sir, colonel, sir!" can scarcely be recorded in mere words. For it was like a sudden monosyllabic shout, making one word of four, a shout that sounded something like "Scurs!" fulfilling its purpose the way a cork does as it pops from the bottle.

All the Powenzes knew how to behave in war. They had a feeling for its grand sentimental possibilities. In short, they obliged it in every way—without ever once taking it seriously.

The plain fact is, however, that although they had been so scurrilously defamed as unpatriotic and disreputable rabble, the entire Powenz pack down to the last man (Jadup and little Jubal excepted) ended up bearing arms at the front, in the infantry, of course—even Zephirin and father Powenz. In the meantime mother Sabina and Lilith looked after the family business.

The family was, said Powenz, practically a small army in itself, which made for infinite possibilities—if they went about things cleverly enough and, as they had always done, presented the world with a united front. And that is what they did.

There is one splendid photograph of the

"Powenz Regiment" as they now and again liked to call themselves in jest, showing all of them in their uniforms of field gray—except for mute Violand, who wears his washable cotton-drill hospital outfit, striped white and blue like a prison uniform. He still looks rather bad and with his gauze turban resembles a captured maharaja. In the center (seated) is full-bearded Baltus Powenz, a homeguard cap on his head and at his feet a barrel with an inscription in chalk that reads: "Password is Home! 14 Days!" To the right and left of it, lying propped on their elbows like the corner statues in the pediment of the Parthenon, are Heinrich and Zephirin. The former has his Red Cross insignia bound on his arm and is unfortunately somewhat out of focus. The others are all standing; Kaspar is easily identified by the strap of his rifle and by the obvious way he has hooked the thumb of his maimed hand into his uniform jacket. It is indeed a picture that epitomizes the valor of the men gathered for it, who display fine military style in each crease of their uniforms, in the sit of their caps. How fine young Zephirin looks in that knightly helmet, in the shade of that gray halo that made every face more handsome!

These six warriors, each with his own peculiarities but all with a strong family resemblance, did indeed build a small brigade of their own. They saw themselves as mercenaries, pure and simple (if at rather meager pay). And if Baltus Powenz had ever been asked what he considered the aims of the war, he would have answered without thinking, hand to his heart, "A house of my own on land of my own!"

Chapter Nine

Ends, despite death and tears,
with consolations

By means of multiple petitions, all disingenuous, the Powenz pack slowly but surely succeeded in building their own brigade.

In a small skirmish near Ferme Trouchy, it was their last-minute action that turned what had begun as a disaster into a victory. The entire affair was even mentioned, with appropriate praise, in an official army report.

This was the heroic battle in the course of which Violand was so badly wounded; nor do I consider it improper to boast that I was a witness, and not an impassive one, I might add, to this incident.

When I first arrived there, Ferme Trouchy was a reddish hill composed of the totally pulverized remains of what had once been lovely bricks. At the edge of town stood an unplaned wooden board bristling with splinters; on it someone had written with indelible pencil in German: "This was Truschi!" Rain had made the violet letters weep violet tears.

At one time there had been some trees that had served as a windbreak on the west side of the barnyard. Now they were naked stumps, like the feet of those immense divine birds of Greek myth that, even after they had been chopped off, still clutched at the earth with their talons. Legend says that these birds had been sleeping in the fields, resembling nothing so much as some strange forest, and that a blasphemer had so mutilated them with his axe that thereafter they flew without rest, forever incapable of returning to earth on their maimed and bloodied stumps.

For a long time this pile of battered brick was crowned with the skeleton of a baby carriage; a tag of white cloth could be seen clinging to it and waving bye-bye in the wind. All around, flat as a frying pan or the surface of the moon, lay the shell-torn countryside. Most of the holes were filled with water and stared back at you like thick eyeglasses rimmed with green. In some of them frogs had made their home, and they would sing on stormy summer evenings.

I also recall that in the false quiet of the days preceding the English reconnaissance in force—in the course of which the Powenzes were to distinguish themselves—flock upon flock of crows flew right across the front lines from morning till night, following some invisible highway of the heavens. Just for fun, an artillery battery threw some shrapnel into the black host. The crows were terrified, and yet they held unswervingly to their course high over the red hill that had once been Ferme Trouchy.

At this point, Violand Powenz was serving as an orderly to a Captain Probst. Violand had all the qualities that make an orderly indispensible. He was sly, resourceful and could not be insulted. He could show deceptively good manners, be clean and tidy, and could create the impression of being absolutely dependable. Above all, he was a joy to behold, so tall and bone-dry. He was considered a charming fellow; all the officers just called him "that nice orderly of Captain Probst's," and they often slipped him cigarettes or even wine—and if they tipped him, they did so generously. You did not feel right if you gave him too little.[11]

The captain was a rather trying man, for in civilian life he was a poet and he frightened easily. When the gods of battle roared, he became terrified, but then he would pull himself together again.

The red hill lay between the first and second lines of battle, and you would think it not worth wasting powder on. But Violand had by chance discovered that there was a little bit of cellar still left intact under the ruins and that it was filled

[11]The power of physiognomic suggestion! (The author).

with vintage wine. It sometimes happened that prior to the German advance, the farmers of an area would wall off a portion of their cellars to make a cache.

Violand had had the good luck of being close by when a shell hit the cellar. He had been busy knocking the copper driving-ring off a dud, a rather dangerous task, after all, since the thing could have gone off at any time. When the red dust had cleared, Violand saw the earth opened before him and, gasping for air, he crawled toward the hole to find better cover. He slid down into the darkness on a small avalanche of stones.

Shining his field-gray flashlight all about him, Violand discovered that he was in a small but well-stocked wine cellar. There was a stupefying odor of ruby-red wine. One of the kegs had been ripped open on one side and dark wine dripped onto the broken floor tiles.

He lapped it up, singing all the while in splendid voice.

There was a cubic yard of red-topped bottles stacked like ammo.

Violand helped himself, and it is to his credit that, even as he sipped, he at once thought of his father, never guessing that he was not far away at all.

Of course Violand carefully blocked the entrance again, so that no one might spy his discovery. He had removed a sample bottle that looked especially promising, and now he disguised it by slipping it into an empty, nondescript artillery shell. It fit perfectly. All dusty, like some walking clay figurine, he returned to his captain, whose anger and concern were easily mollified.

Father Powenz, who was doing very well working in a supply convoy, made a detour to visit his sons in the trenches—the once fat Fabian, Violand and Zephirin, and gentle Heinrich, too, whom he found busy delousing his shirt, a raven perched on his shoulder.

But, oh, he did not kill a single one of the repulsive creatures; instead, he gathered them up in a little box in order later to set them free somewhere where nothing could happen to them.

Zephirin occupied himself with drawing pictures, either of his comrades from life or simple sketches of graves for survivors.

For the most part Fabian slept. But his dreams were not quite as happy as they once had been in peacetime, when, after all, he had not been forced to sleep in a military uniform and boots.

One dream, however, had pursued him for a long, long time, he said.

His dream was that he was out on a secret patrol, crawling on his belly through a tangle of barbed wire in which roses were blooming and where painted tin birds—the kind you wind up—

Heinrich Powenz

had their rusty nests. He met an Englishman who, like a reptile, was slowly and agonizingly crawling on all fours, just as Fabian was. They were both naked. And now, thought Fabian, quickly thumbing through his beginner's gunnery manual, now, sad to say, I guess I'll have to kill him. And slowly he took aim. The other man, likewise leafing through a little blue book, took aim too. But now the figure changed its shape. First he was a black Negro, then suddenly became a red Indian with a warbonnet of bright feathers. All at once, however, he turned white, and Fabian was terrified. Now the man he was aiming at was himself. No doubt of it: Fabian was about to shoot Fabian. Just at this ticklish moment, the enemy opened fire and filled Fabian with several holes; Fabian returned fire, but flinched and held his eyes shut with every shot. But his gun did not work. He had forgotten to take off the safety. He stood there laughing and bleeding from his many wounds; he cheerfully reached out to shake hands with his enemy, who was also laughing and who began to drink the blood as if from a fountain. Then they exchanged weapons as a token of mutual respect.

"Almost, all but, very nearly," Fabian said and raised a finger in warning, and then he awoke.

The brothers were honestly worried for their oversized father.

"You have so much surface area, Baltus," Violand noted with disapproval, and he was happy only when he knew that his father was back in safe territory. But first he had to show him, from a distance at least, the red hill and reveal the secret of what was hidden inside it. He gave him a couple of bottles of the treasure he had extracted thus far and promised him more soon.

That same evening, however, the English began their surprise reconnaissance in force, during which the Germans unfortunately lost the red hill to them. Violand, having rescued his poetic captain (whose wounds, however, proved fatal), turned back once more to fetch the poor man's binoculars. A piece of shrapnel struck him in the head, and there he now lay, not moving a muscle, stretched out beside the red hill, binoculars in hand. No one could help him, since the English had advanced clear up to the second line of battle.

At the time, Baltus Powenz was sitting next to Kaspar, who had once again returned to the front despite his wounded hand (rumor had it on account of pretty Madame Robinot). They were drinking red wine when the lightly wounded men who were falling back told them the news of the "bloody mess" up front and of Violand's death— for it was assumed that he had fallen.

In war, the wilder the confusion, the better the man who keeps a really clear head can follow through on his intentions. As happened now with

Powenz. He told Kaspar that, cost what it might, he would go get Violand (who was his favorite son) in order, as he put it, to bury him with his own hands—this latter apparently growing out of some special sense of ritual fitness. Kaspar agreed wholeheartedly; they grabbed their weapons and started forward.

From the pothole where I was crouched, I saw them coming. They were both, to be frank, really quite drunk. They advanced in step, undaunted and singing with round, open mouths, "Then sweetheart, do not weep and do not cry, don't make this soldier's heart the heavier."

They were so soused they were simply immune to death.

I shall never forget the sight of that great man marching toward me like some heathen god, his helmet wreathed in green leaves, in his hand a sapling for a staff (and nothing could have induced him to sacrifice his flowing beard to the confines of a gas mask.) His kith and kin rallied round him—Fabian, now grown rather lean; Zephirin, a mere child; and Heinrich the medic—all ready to do reverence to Violand, to bear him home dead or alive.

All on their own, they began the counterattack; in a surprise move they closed off the trenches and then swept them free of bewildered Englishmen in a ruthless and overwhelming display of hand-grenade firepower. Powenz tossed those English helmets around—were they shaving bowls á la Don Quixote?—like so many paper plates. Wugg the raven nose-dived for the English sergeant's face; he hacked and clawed and crowed hurrah. Finally they freed Violand, still alive.

It was almost morning as, with great wailing, they brought him home, wrapped in a brown tarp and lashed to a pole the way hunters used to carry a slain deer or the way the scouts Joshua and Caleb brought home giant grapes out of the land of Canaan. (He did recover, as I said, though only very slowly, and he was mute his whole life long.) And on their shoulders they bore yet another burden hung from a pole. But just for show. There was no man inside, though a pair of mud-caked boots did stick out at the end of the tarp. The Powenzes had stuffed the uniform of a dead soldier with wine bottles from the cellar on the red hill, and so with no interference they rescued the camouflaged treasure that had almost been lost.

At risk of life and limb, they made three trips to bear the precious load home; it tinkled softly as they marched in step.

And so, the red hill was recaptured. We have the Powenz pack to thank for this remarkable deed; they fought for private ends but with faultless infantry tactics. Another fact, however, ought not be left totally unmentioned—I mean the author's effective support of this effort, which contributed considerably to its victorious outcome. And certainly brave Baltus Powenz would be able to confirm my contention without further ado, had he not been so suddenly and unexpectedly taken from us by that flaming meteor.

Chapter Ten

Which dare not be suppressed

Some time before, Frau Sabina had received a confidential letter from her husband by military post; in it he stated as a foregone conclusion that the war would soon end—and not happily. Among other things, he wrote, "From here on out, dear wife of mine, keep supplies on hand of red flags and of black-red-gold ones. But take good care of the old black-white-red-ones, too; there will be need of them at some point later on as well. Halt production of all generals and monarchs." (As we know, they made pretty little plaster casts of them.) "At most, perhaps a few more Hindenburgs. But get rid of the pictures of the kaiser as fast as you can for whatever price you can get."

Worthy Frau Powenz did as she was bidden. And so it happened that the revolution did not take her by surprise. She was at once in the happy position of being able to meet her new customers' needs in the most enterprising, if opportunistic, fashion.

Chapter Eleven

The grand misconception

At war's end, the Powenz brigade separated itself from the mighty throng and returned to its native soil. Undefeated in battle, they now resembled some wild, piratical nomad horde as they gathered picturesquely around their packwagon, accompanied by dogs, cats, goats and a lovely French calf named Madeleine. They were tanned bronze and were wise in the way of the world.

Powenz could not be disuaded from also using this occasion to import a few fine enemy bricks into Germany. In purely national terms—let us be clear on this—Baltus Powenz felt himself to be a citizen of the land of humanity. He saw national borders only as a kind of local color, and he enjoyed maps primarily for their pictorial qualities.

He never doubted that he was a good German, a fact of which he was neither ashamed nor of which he would have thought to boast, seeing that he was quite innocent in the matter. It was, however, a principle with him never to serve any nation—if anything, the nation should extend its services to him. For the most part, he forwent the pleasure as best he could.

His dream was one day to have an independent island, Powenz Island, that he could call his own, a kind of family kingdom where he, Baltus I, would rule as the glorious king of the Powenzians, lord of his own house and father of a mighty people yet to be born. It was for that he lived, for that he had gone to war as well—though to be sure he firmly resolved to make the war serve his purposes, too.

And while millions of Germans lost the war, as far as Baltus Powenz was concerned, he had won it.

As might be expected, it took only the rumor that the Powenz pack, armed to the teeth and in company with a troop of savage rebels, was approaching on Kyps Road to set the population of Moessel in desperate panic. For there were many who had not been exactly friendly to the Powenzes in peacetime and whose consciences were not especially good.

The lovely Lilith Powenz was pumped by her disconcerted neighbors about what her brothers might possibly be up to. She gave them a taunting shrug of the shoulders.

"According to the official report," she said offhandedly, "a small but terrible army has banded together around my dear family. Most of them are hungry and thirsty, all are rash young fellows, deserters, tramps, rascals, some thieves, of course, and perhaps a murderer or two. But what's the difference—our consciences are clear. We'll all see what happens soon enough."

The upshot of this dubious answer was that a half hour later Surveyor Knipfel hurriedly left town, his face darkly hidden in a heavy black beard. But Herr Gockeley stayed—having checked his pistols.

Lilith walked over to the ropemaker's as conspicuously as possible and bought lots of rope— which, just as she had hoped, was soon known all over town. It was now clear why the night before several lamp posts had been hung with neat little placards reading Reserved for Knipfel, or Airy Spot for Dattel.

The townspeople closed up shop.

Traffic, already rather light, grew lighter still and finally ceased altogether. Anxious eyes kept close watch on Kyps Road.

The fact is that in those days, any relatively energetic man with a handful of adventurous soldiers could have struck terror in the heart of a town like Moessel. For these "old biddy towns," as Powenz scornfully liked to call them, had already seen too much hunger and were painfully weary of war. They would have put up with almost anything.

184

Only the three old sisters, Katharina, Ernestina and little Babette, still kept their nails untrimmed so that in an emergency they could scratch all the better. They now set water to boiling in great pots, intending to pour it on the heads of advancing rebels should any dare threaten them with bodily harm. Also at the ready was a large supply of pepper they had hoarded, for strewing in the eyes of would-be attackers. And with a wicked laugh, Katharina brought out a bottle of hydrochloric acid.

It was nearly evening before the Powenz pack marched into town, but as with everything this eccentric family did, they were magnificently organized. At the fore ran all the children from the village of Kyps, whom Baltus Powenz had bribed with candy, something they had long had to do without. Each child carried a banner, and a lad named Baptist, who had unmistakably Powenzian traits (apparently one of Kaspar's illegitimate sons, or perhaps even of father Powenz himself), constantly fired his little pals on, leading them in chorus with shouts of "One, two, three, hurrah!"

Then, a bit tipsy as always and with his helmet wreathed in oak leaves, came Baltus Powenz riding a horse arrayed with flowers. After him came little Jadup, beating incessantly on a drum; then, led by Vice-sergeant-major Kaspar Powenz, came Fabian, Zephirin, mute Violand (his head still bandaged) and Heinrich—all at stiff attention, their ranks closed and weapons shouldered. Violand's wound, by the way, had long since healed, but he had used a little red ink on the bandage to simulate some poignant bloodstains. At the rear were more children, running in triumph, yowling and waving little flags that bore the colors of Germany—and of all the rest of the nations of Europe.

The wagonload of booty, however, had been left with Frau Sabina's parents, where Heinrich's pet French cow, the goats and Wugg the faithful raven had also been deposited.

Frau Sabina herself, supported on Lilith's arm and holding the hand of infant Jubal, the youngest Powenz of all, waited expectantly in the market place for the arrival of the little parade. There, in full view of the townsfolk who had now gathered, their fears banished, Baltus Powenz swung down from his horse and rushed into the open arms of his wife—after first tossing back the reins with a grand gesture so that Baptist might hold his charger.

The Powenzes, man and wife, lay silent in one another's arms.

Kaspar shouted, "Attention!" Jadup gave a roll on his drum.

Then their father addressed his brave sons in a smart military oration, recalling both their wounds

186

and the medals so justly bestowed upon them, while clearly intimating that these heroic sons of Germany were not being accorded the honor due them by their country. He spoke of four long years of sticking one's neck out in a world full of enemies; spoke of the knife in the back and of incompetent diplomats. But in his peroration, he returned to call for a cheer to be raised in honor of his wife, who had "faithfully persevered in the bosom of her family"—and the cheer went up from those who stood assembled, mostly young scamps and scalawags.

The ceremonies were ended with a loud salute fired into the red twilight sky toward all four points of the compass and with a violent display of signal flares and rockets, all of which mightily frightened many an honest citizen, hiding behind locked shutters and doors and who knew nothing of the peaceful intent behind this display.

"Look, there it is," said Frau Quiebus, turning pale, "they're setting up their barricades! Bloodiest civil war is upon us! I heard the drums. By midnight we shall all be dangling from the lampposts."

"It seems to me," said Edwin mischievously, "that for people like us they'll at least first lower the lampposts before they hoist us up."

Frau Quiebus found the remark impudent and heartless.

"You have no moral seriousness, Edwin," she said. "Just listen, they've already started shooting again."

Out on the marketplace, the merry cracking and popping was in full swing, and the children yelled, "One, two, three, hurrah!" But it all sounded very different on Luisen Strasse, where no one guessed that it was all merely in honor of the festive entry of the Powenz pack.

Quite the opposite. There was talk that there had been a dozen slain, that the mayor had been taken prisoner and was in danger of being executed under martial law, that drunken irregulars had already begun to plunder—in their vanguard, of course, the Powenz pack—that no mercy was being shown.

"It was awful enough that we were led to believe that revolution had broken out," said Frau Quiebus proudly when the whole affair turned out to be perfectly harmless. "It would have been just like the fiends, you know."

She just simply did not like the Powenzes.

BOOK
OF EDIFICATION

Tantum est hoc regnum
quod regibus imperat ipsis.

Its power is so great
that even kings are subject to it.

—*Manilius*

Chapter One

Is devoted principally to lazy Fabian—
To be read at bedtime

There was general public amazement that upon returning home the Powenz pack showed no Spartacist appetites whatever. Powenz was quite impervious to all political blandishments, whether of the right or the left. He stated frankly that he knew how to defend himself and his family in the event of their endangerment by a putsch, whatever quarter it might come from. The name Powenz, he declared, was a party designation in and of itself.

Nor did these good folk so much as consider handing in their weapons as was officially requested. They even owned a machine gun. It was long a mystery just where and how they managed to hide the thing every time the house was subjected to a thorough search. Only recently did Zephirin reveal to me that the strange and mythic stuffed beast that was set out for all to see on a shelf in the hall—looking much like a sea-cow, I thought—harbored the machine gun within it.

Each of the various political parties, however,

constantly attempted to enlist the Powenzes in its ranks—if only for reasons of sheer numbers. At last Baltus came up with an excellent idea. Considering just how many Powenzes there were, after all, they could have a representative in every party. They drew lots. And drowsy Fabian had to join the extreme right, while gentle Heinrich became a communist.

And so all factions were lent a helping hand.

I know another family where the same thing happened. They were all honorable men and good Germans, and they all lived to a ripe old age.

Baltus Powenz, however, quite justifiably termed his family the ethnic minority of Moessel.

During these years of political ignominy, patriotic factionalism and human need, the Powenzes naturally had to employ all the forces at their disposal to make an economic go of things. And it is indeed touching to think of how they drove themselves, each trying to earn money in his own way, each possessed by the same goal: the house.

Our Fabian, for example, had visions of engaging in some sort of passive work, not unlike that of a clock weight whose productivity is in its mass. This alone seemed to him worth pursuing.

His father had had to reprimand him often enough, pointing out that his dreams were generally unprofitable. But it was in a dream that Fabian came up with a plan that soon proved especially beneficial. He dreamt he met an angel who assured him that he stood in particular favor with the god of sleep; and when he awakened from this vision, it seemed to him that there was more sense in it than in any other verity, human or divine.

He decided from that moment on to dedicate his life to the nurture of sleep and rest, to the cultivation of dreams. Above all, he hoped to live from what he earned by sleeping. One night when Heinrich could not sleep, Fabian dictated to him from a dream the sensational pamphlet "The Blessings of a Just Sleep," in which he passionately, insistently professed and argued his thesis: "The Lord provides for His own while they sleep."

It was as good as a new religion, no doubt of it, and—just as Fabian had intended—it therefore found both bitter enemies and faithful adherents. Fabian followed up with several wild tracts, e.g., "The Kingdom of Heaven Cometh Only to Sleepers," "Dreams, the Gifts of God," "Is Work a Sin?" and "Ecclestiastical Sleep, an Eschatological Interpretation." Violand, too, knew his scriptures, and under the assumed name of P. Valerian Zump was commissioned to write a brochure in spiritual rebuttal. He succeeded admirably, since he felt a total lack of interest in the matter.

And so Fabian rendered devout service to the god of sleep, and he had nothing against the fact

Aurora
An original painting by Zephirin Powenz
(In the possession of the town of Moessel)

that his small band of followers were called The Sect of the Seven Sleepers—it was good publicity and detracted hardly at all. A rich American lady settled a pension on him, and, as unbelievable as it may sound, large donations came in from near and far for the Holy Archsleeper, allowing Fabian not only to live out his dream with no cares, but also to contribute considerable sums toward the building of the house.

In his "Doctrine of a Sleep Pleasing Unto God," Fabian had convincingly demonstrated that, just as one can pray for others, he was capable of sleeping for others. He called it "sleeping in God," or hypnotheism, and he would do his best in return for a voluntary contribution defraying the expenses of the World Federation of Pious Sleepers. He ran a small but flourishing business on the side, too, interpreting dreams on the basis of "Hopkin's Hypnopsychic Method"—so ran the clever ads. Hundreds of inquiries poured in.

All of this, naturally, was not carried out under the name of Powenz, which was already notorious enough as it was. The advertisements were signed with a code number, while the signature on the pious tracts was the very simple and intimate "Brother Fabian."

He had the unexpected pleasure of discovering that Frau Quiebus was also to be found among the many persons who wrote the institute to have their often highly amusing dreams interpreted. He was able to provide her with a downright and infernally malicious interpretation of both her personality and her fate.

In an extended oration, father Powenz praised his son, extolling his distinguished achievement on behalf of the family, but Fabian soon fell asleep again and heard neither good nor evil.

It was lazy Fabian's habit always to sleep in a light robe—his dream robe, as he called this magic nocturnal outfit, which had had its beginnings in a simple kind of nightshirt that his mother had mended and darned several hundred times with bright stitches and loud patches.[12] This evolved into a garment embroidered with softest silk, and as the sect started to turn a tidy profit, Fabian laid in a large supply of them. He gave each one a nickname, like "Orange Blossom" or "Sweet Dreamsies" or "Pale Moonica" or "Nox Nebulus," and they were bespangled with flowers, stars, girls, animals, gods and even with verses—all gifts from the so-called Dream Ladies, the faithful devotees of his wonderful doctrine of Sleep Pleasing unto God.

Fabian was, by the way, at least conscientious enough to write the names of the believers for whose souls he had been bidden to sleep (the so-

[12]The original garment can now be found in the costume collection of the Powenz Museum.

called telesomnia) on a piece of paper and slip it under his pillow. In the end he even began to believe that these poor petitioners were being helped; that without his ever feeling it, he took upon himself their cares, their unhappy loves, and above all, their sickness and insomnia. He believed it because of the proof of countless unsolicited letters of gratitude that arrived daily. Miss A.W. from Z. (a forty-one-year-old clerk) wrote that thanks to the telesomnia he had performed for her, she had recovered her lost youth. Another lady, who had visited some twenty-one medical specialists over the years, expressed her gratitude for his having slept away her chronic stomach problems; a retired colonel from B. was grateful for the same effect on a stubborn case of sciatica. And although it was a rather expensive procedure, he was frequently asked to perform a Sleep of Bliss (particularly useful in affairs of the heart and for childless couples).

It goes without saying that as a matter of deepest conviction, Fabian loathed all those people who, simply because they cannot sleep, think they have to wake up their fellow man at five in the morning while claiming that nothing is healthier than rising early. Strangely enough, this great snorer always passionately denied that he snored. But his brothers proved it to him by making a gramophone recording of him asleep and then playing it back for him.

Sleeping Robe
worn by Fabian Powenz himself
(Powenz Museum, Hall V, case 2)

Chapter Two

"To the Fine Arts"

Merry Zephirin may well be one of the most important personalities of the Powenz clan. His genial talent for drawing developed splendidly. He was an untiring scenic designer. He had an eye for the picturesque, and his constant care was to provide a convincing artistic backdrop for all Powenzian enterprises.

His hair was a mane of wild curls; he wore a broad-brimmed hat and an artist's black scarf that floated gently on the wind. His every word, his every pose was that of an artist. There he stood, tall and gaunt and creative, his clothes fluttering about him as if some invisible angel were always at his back puffing at them.

Of course he scrupulously saw to all the painting that needed to be done at home. But if the least bit of paint was left over (his preference was for brick red), he would start brushing it on whatever got in his way. He was unmerciful and gave his brothers no end of trouble.

"I'd say the beds could use it," he would say

199

and terrorize the family by painting away until there was not a drop left in his can.

I am in no position to serve as an interpreter of Zephirin's artistry. I am not an art historian. It is only as a layman that I refer here to this young indigenous artist's rough folkloristic originality, a quality that makes his tender genre paintings so charming. The ease of his brushwork, the accuracy of detail, the delightful sweetness of his colors—all deserve highest praise. I do not presume to set myself up as a judge, but I have yet to see another portrait of a woman at once so realistic and yet idealistic as that from Zephirin's hand. Another overwhelming proof for his mastery of his art is his growing number of commissions. In his own modest way, he humorously refers to himself as a "painter of kitsch"!

Chapter Three

Or, footsteps overhead

Man was not made for all work and no play.
One day a report that aroused general excitement made the rounds—the three maiden sisters
would at any moment be receiving a charming
visitor. And indeed a fiery young lady from the
Rhineland named Jakobina Haas moved in with
them. No one had seen her as yet, not even Jadup,
for the sly old ladies kept too close a watch on her.

From that point, the older Powenz boys, especially Kaspar, slept very fitfully; they moaned and
even wept in their sleep. For Jakobina lived in the
room above their heads, and they could hear her
virginal steps as she walked gracefully about. They
heard her when she washed and they heard her
bed creak when she crawled into it.

Violand penned a sonnet to his invisible love.
Fabian had very vivid dreams about her and sang
the praises of how sweet and delicate she was, like
the brush of a butterfly's wings; he described her
eyes in minutest poetic detail and also the color,
size, shape and strength of her mouth; and then,

ah, how strange, he said that her limbs were tanned brown but that her torso was white as... he could not say how white. Even Heinrich's eyes grew larger.

Once, shortly after midnight, Kaspar rose from his bed and, dressed just as he was, shimmied up the gutter spout.

The girl upstairs awoke with alarm as he entered. But she had heard many fine things about him and had herself seen him once before. She angrily told him to leave at once—but whispered and listened anxiously if perhaps the old ladies had not heard something as well.

They had—and swore terrible revenge on this bold pirate of love.

Lilith Quiebus, née Powenz
Dr. Edwin Quiebus
as newlyweds

Chapter Four[13]

And now I must relate the dreadful vengeance the three old maids wreaked on Kaspar. They lay in ambush until, all unsuspecting, he once again climbed up to Jakobina. The conniving old ladies had locked the poor girl in her closet.

Kaspar was stark naked as he sprang into the darkened room, and before he knew what was happening, he had been tied in loops of clothesline. Though he cursed and struck wildly at the old women, they had him in their clutches and threw him onto the bed.

"Now I've got you, my sweet little dove. Come to me now at last, my pretty," one old hag mocked and then kissed him tenderly with her bitter mouth.

Oh, and how they snuggled up to him and teased him, jabbing him with their cold pointed noses, biting him with their false teeth! He received such a terrible shock that he was unable to

[13]Owing to many requests, the chapter which follows has been omitted.

make love for a whole six months afterwards. For the old ladies beat him with nettles and were disgustingly naughty to him. He only wanted to die right then and there rather than endure their infernal sport. The worst was Babette, the youngest of the crones, who still had her hopes and dressed herself up like a flirty teenager with lots of pink ribbons. Her behavior was absolutely odious, all languorous looks and giggles. She pinched his cheeks, petted and teased him, called him her sweetie and honeylamb, until finally the enraged Kaspar recovered his manly strength and ripped off his bonds. Up he sprang from his bed of involuntary debauchery and using the tattered clothesline, he lashed away at the wrinkled old temptresses, who fled with loud screeches. At last he escaped through the window.

For days on end Jakobina wept for him, but he never returned.

Chapter Five

Written with a reluctant pen

Since I want to give a truthful picture of the Powenz clan, I dare not suppress the things of which cruel Jadup was guilty in the days before he himself was smitten by one of Cupid's arrows.

I know of no one else whom total strangers would invite at the drop of a hat to join them for an automobile ride, a camping trip, a tour. But they would invite charming Jadup.

A highly respectable aristocratic family—consisting of a count, his wife, daughter and son—fell head over heels in love with our Jadup and kindly invited him to join them on an extended trip.

The count outfitted him with clothes, the countess wept with him, the daughter loved him and young Count Johann idolized him.

One may, of course, think what one will about love's strange enchantments and peculiar aberrations, but in my judgment Jadup's behavior in this instance can only be strongly condemned. He shamelessly invited each member of the whole infatuated family up to his room late one night, just to have the pleasure of watching the explosion when they all bumped into one another. But though painfully embarrassed, the members of the family forgave each other and joined together to boot the villain out of the house.

The mockery and scorn that Jadup displayed toward all those who were unfortunate enough to fall in love with him finally annoyed the god of love. What if he should blind this heartless lad, if he should make him fall suddenly and madly in love? What if the offended divinity were to punish this boy—who had so enthusiastically made fools of others, sported with them without once feeling a tug at his heart—by letting *him* suffer the agonies of love?

At the very start of these reflections, I suggested that natural forces were apparently no longer sufficient to tame this heathen. And so it does not seem out of place for me to see the god Eros in the form of a mysterious, terrifying young man who landed—hardly by chance—with his large yellow balloon in an idyllic clearing of the Powder Woods near Kyps.

I call him a god because he came from on high.

He suddenly floated down out of the clear blue sky in his reed basket, much as if he had been brought in a lady's handbag from the moon—or from a dress ball. He landed in the midst of wild-flowers and grasses; and like the dress of a beautiful woman, the empty sack of the balloon billowed and rippled gracefully, then sank down onto the meadow.

Jadup—and this, too, must give one pause—was the first to arrive at the spot on his bike. He rode up just at the moment when the strange god climbed out of the basket.

My assumption that this newcomer's sole intention was to punish Jadup is, of course, purely hypothetical. But Baltus Powenz was also of the opinion that this handsome stranger from Berlin must have cast some secret spell over his son. Beyond that, however, Baltus did not believe that he was that ancient deity whom mankind has so unjustly forgotten, but rather he thought of him as a common, ordinary swindler or confidence man.

The fact is that shortly thereafter, the fellow flew off again in his balloon, taking along Jadup, who overnight had developed an abject, fawning attachment for him. As if borne by the moon, Jadup floated heavenwards with his idol, up and away from Moessel.

The Powenz family, normally anything but prudish, disapproved of this totally unprofitable madness on Jadup's part; they applied to him all kinds of ugly names, which for decency's sake I shall omit.

The retribution of the gods, however, was

terrible, for the very moment Jadup fell in love, he lost all his charm for others.

The last time I saw him, he was walking the hot streets of Berlin with a painful smile on his lips and pebbles in his shoes—his amused master was now tormenting him as he had once tormented others.

He has become, by the way, a very popular quick-change artist and bird-call imitator. But he is said to be forever in the midst of an unhappy love affair, to be incredibly sentimental and dreadfully jealous. What a shame, considering his talents!

This, then, was Jadup's fate. But what of Lilith's?

One must keep in mind that Lilith was a sorceress, at least if one is to believe the manifold rumors about her that are current even now.[14] Her reputation was very bad—and not just because a good many young men in Moessel were much too bold in advertising how they had tasted her sweetest favors (and with no justification for such boasts whatever, as I shall prove), nor simply because it was said that she made fools of the most venerable graybeards—no, it was because it was generally reported that she lived from love, that her love could be bought!

---

[14]The climate of Moessel is known worldwide for its tendency to further the building of myths.

Unfortunately, there were good grounds for assuming that of an evening Lilith Powenz received very frequent visits from young gentlemen; and I must admit that this fact distressed me greatly, especially since these gentlemen were most certainly not to my taste.

"I do not understand you at all, Lilith," I said to her disapprovingly—and the right to address her by her first name marked the fullest extent of the favors she permitted me. "I really don't understand you; you had me turned away from the door yesterday so you could spend the evening with that disgusting, repulsive Doctor Gilpin."

"Easy does it!" said Lilith with an amused, knowing look. "What do you know about it? Just between us, I can't stand him or any of the others who come to see me. You can be absolutely certain that I don't love any of them. I'd much rather love you, dear sweet author of mine. But if I told you the whole truth, you're so silly you wouldn't believe a word of it. So now go, because today Herr..." (and she quickly looked in her little book) "Herr Gluecklein is coming to see me."

Gluecklein! Him too! The rich, beastly owner of the auto-repair shop!

All these rascals spent their evenings in Lilith's unusual room.

Her room revealed what could be called a genius for bad taste. As I found out later, however, the effect was intentional, the product of many hilarious evenings during which the design had been conceived by Fabian and then carried out with the help of Zephirin, the house artist. It included dusty "arrangements" of peacock feathers, Jerusalem cherries and straw flowers behind an elaborate mirror, in the frame of which was stuck an expensive collection of dreadfully sentimental and tasteless postcards. A female nude with vesuvian illumination adorned the long wall above the sky-blue bed, at the head of which stood a little Raphaelesque angel holding its head in its hands. The vanity table was equally hideous and glittered with lots of bottles of repulsive cheap perfume. Fans had been inserted in the tortoise-shell frames of photographs of notorious men-about-town. I only learned later that Violand had taken great pains to acquire them from the Moessel Studio of Photography, just so he could put the final touch on the boudoir's questionable atmosphere. There was also a beribboned guitar, and a large empty Italian wine bottle in its wicker basket—plus a pair of fancy dolls set amid the divan's garishly loud pillows. The lighting each evening was, of course, unrelievedly saccharine.

The table was set for two with showy china; but there was also a simple tin coinbox in the shape of a house, similar to the ones that used to be set out in country inns when a collection was being taken up for building a new village church.

Only recently did I discover what a devil Lilith

really was—though with extenuating circumstances. I report what follows with reservation and only because I am committed to pass on all information that serves to illuminate the character of the persons of my tale. I do not in the least mean to exonerate or excuse the actions of this bizarre young girl.

Lilith Powenz had learned from her father how to concoct a potion that, so she claimed, was made of harmless ingredients but had a quick and sure effect. According to her, this magic potion was a very powerful tranquilizer. Baltus Powenz allegedly had the recipe from a Greek monk, and he himself told me that he had successfully used it on unwelcome rival suitors many a time; for he maintained, the drug could totally numb all amatory desires for several hours.

It is clear that someone would have to have a diabolical heart to mix this potion into the food that an unsuspecting lover would then eat—and, even worse, to watch as the love-crazed man suffered the pangs of helpless shame and impotence.

Jadup knew about all this—naturally. And according to him, his sister would secretly gloat over her victim's lack of vigor, all the while dissembling in the vilest way. First she would console him with soft and sympathetic words, and then tease him by playing the spurned woman who had been deeply hurt. But since she had mixed the magic potion with the food or wine, she got her share of it, too. From a legal point of view, this dangerous sport can only be termed an attempt to inflict grievous bodily harm. At best it can be explained, if not excused, by what was doubtless this girl's unusually strongly developed sense of family patriotism. This trait, which Edwin Quiebus—who so often found just the right word for things—once quite aptly called "powenzialistic extremism," was common to all Powenzes; but none had inherited it in such passionate form as Lilith.

She, too, was rushing headlong toward her fate.

Which is to say, toward the enemy, Edwin Quiebus. Caught between love and hate, she had never forgotten him since the day of the bite. One evening he arrived quite unexpectedly to apologize for a friend who could not keep his appointment. With all sorts of shameless airs and odious theatrics, she invited him in to stay. He stayed, and with a heavy heart, yet one filled with a sweet foreboding. He sat down at the table. But just as he was about to take a bite of food, Lilith remembered—and pushed the table over, smashing plates and bowls. And in words that at first were those of anger, then of great passion, and finally of deepest emotion, she opened her heart to this sensitive man—and he listened with unbelieving joy.

And so it happened that the blood of enemies

was mixed—though no one was to know about it at first.

But it should be noted here that later this secret alliance also led to permanent peace between Baltus Powenz and Thusnelda Quiebus.

Malicious tongues have even claimed that the irresistible old man was seen billing and cooing with that colossal lady.

I can most definitely state that such was not the case. On the contrary, only after many fainting spells and tantrums did Frau Quiebus, bitter adversary of all the Powenzes that she was, surrender her sensitive, learned son to savage Lilith.

Chapter Six

Is recommended as worthy of emulation

Baltus Powenz was, to be sure—should one wish to put it that way—a kind of war profiteer. For the first time he could remember, he had no debts. He had even built up a little capital in Swiss francs and American dollars, which, as the German mark began to lose value, he now multiplied through all sorts of clever transactions.

In difficult times, he liked to say, a certain disreputability represents a kind of credit that cannot be underestimated. People expect you to turn a dirty profit—and so they do business with you.

And so it came about in those years of penny billionaires, that even reputable citizens, muffled up sometimes beyond all recognition, would seek out Herr Powenz by night. He would always serve them well, and when the deal was closed, grin broadly at his incognito partner and say, "And a good night to you, Your Honor," or "Hope you sleep well tonight, Herr Councilman," or "See you soon, Herr Surveyor."

During this period, our Fabian had to do a

215

dreadful amount of arithmetic. Always seated next to him, however, was one of his brothers, who tickled, pinched and cursed him to keep him awake, for everything now depended on his high-speed calculations.

Nor did a heavily veiled colossus of a woman fail to appear, causing the room to rumble with her steps. She was accompanied by her maid, and in a disguised voice she expressed her wishes in regard to currency. But as she departed, Powenz bowed low and called after her: "My pleasure. And a very good evening to you, Frau Quiebus."

"Woe is me, I've been recognized," he heard her say to her maid.

The basis of Powenz's capital was a government loan meant to help him build his house, which, thanks to good connections, he quickly converted into foreign currency and then repaid with only a few pfennigs. To this was added the profit from a business enterprise of almost criminal cleverness, based once again on an idea of that arch-sleeper, Brother Fabian.

Chapter Seven

Is no less so

One day toward the end of the war, the community of Moessel on the Maar had followed the example of other towns and issued emergency currency. These notes were intended to help solve the problem of a general lack of coins and were of some artistic merit. There were small denominations worth twenty-five and fifty pfennigs, designed by a Munich artist, and they were a joy to every collector's heart.

On the first bill was a view of the town of Moessel as seen from the south, faithfully rendered in an antique style and including the Maar (designated as *marus flumen*) with lots of ships. The railroad was visible as well, and high among the clouds floated a balloon decorated with a little flag. The other bill displayed the Queen Luise Monument (by Bernauer) and a bold portrait of Mayor Dattel, whose signature among those of the other guarantors was pleasantly conspicuous for its childlike legibility.

217

Originating in times of a more solid currency, these municipal banknotes had now, of course, completely lost all value, and there were not a few wags who claimed they were going to paper their walls with them. Indeed, things came to such a pass that the city sold an entire bale of them as wastepaper, and following Fabian's suggestion, Powenz purchased this bale "for a song."

Shortly after the mark finally stabilized, there suddenly appeared in the *Moessel Courier* and in the *Daily News* cleverly worded ads—all apparently by different authors—stating a willingness to pay good money for any and all Moessel banknotes, Series A, brown and blue.

The people of Moessel are not stupid. Their heritage is North German, and they are sharp thinkers. To use the language of the hunt, they have what is commonly called a good nose.

"Aha!" these sly folks said to one another, and the Powenzes heard it all with their own ears. "Aha! That's the way the wind blows!"

And immediately there were whisperings about revaluation and rumors that the members of the town council were secretly buying up the bills, using straw men as their agents and hoping to be rich once the official ordinance was enacted.

"What those big shots can do," grumbled Powenz everywhere he went, "we poor average joes can do, too. That's what I say. Friends, I'm holding on to my browns, you bet I am! Revaluation! Savvy?"

But soon he was forced "by adversity" to sell off part of his unfortunately "rather small" stock at half-price, i.e., at enticingly low rates. People were quick to come to his aid.

The real boom, however, began when the mayor issued an official proclamation declaring these totally irresponsible rumors concerning an alleged revaluation of Municipal Emergency Notes absolute fabrications and myths. The town had no such intention whatsoever, and the authorities were neither legally required to do so nor was there a mechanism by which it could be done.

Was there ever more certain proof that something was up? Hallo! Just look at those slyboots. Well, well, we'll get ours, even if we have to squeeze it out of them!

The whole Powenz pack was busy as never before. They bought the bills back and then resold them at a profit. Then they organized a massive protest demonstration by the citizens of Moessel against "official usury." This resulted in a defiant resolution stating that the citizenry would neither rest nor sleep until their more than just demand for the revaluation of all Municipal Emergency Notes, Series A (brown and blue) be complied with in full. Signed: Knust, convention chairman. On that memorable day, fifty-pfennig bills were going for up to two marks.

Except for a dozen or so bills in especially good condition (which he knew to have some worth as collector's items or perhaps even with a view to their position in the future Powenz Family Museum), Baltus Powenz now sold off his entire holdings and sounded the trumpet for "halt!"—so went his military metaphor.

The mad preference of illusion to reality had spread like a plague among the overwrought citizens of Moessel.

There is documented proof that honest shoemakers, tailors and confectioners now forked up their last bit of hard cash, which they had held tightly onto all through the war, for these worthless scraps of paper, and also that during this time the well-guarded virtue of many a virgin wavered at the sight of a few brown bills.

It was all to the good that, once they had been rudely awakened, no one suspected who was actually at the bottom of it all.

In addition to Fabian, mute Violand made a significant contribution to the success of this enterprise, for he was the author of the inflammatory calls to arms and provocative handbills directed both for and against revaluation. He was a verita-

View of Hall II of the Powenz Museum
in Moessel on the Maar

ble master-chef when it came to public opinion—
he could heat it up, make it bubble, boil and cool
back down just as the moment demanded.

Meanwhile the Powenzes were wise to go on
living their simple, honest life within their four
walls just as before and with no ostentation, despite all the money they had made. Conditions
were rather cramped because of the carefully
stacked bricks, now numbering in the thousands
and taking up a room and a half. But father
Powenz continued to collect them with his own
hands and number them in sequence.

No one yet suspected his prosperity. It seemed
to him that discretion and angelic patience were
the best means by which to let the fruit ripen.

Chapter Eight

In which an uncle in America is heard from

In those days Uncle Melchior, the untiring world traveler, was underway in America, still indefatigably siring black, white and yellow Powenzes, and so it happened that one day Herr Powenz was politely summoned to the Town Hall in order to receive what was termed a highly important, indeed momentous message. Although mother Sabina wept and pleaded with her spouse not to go—she feared they would detain him there for good—Baltus washed and shaved and, in this almost unrecognizable state, marched off with a firm step. Mayor Dattel was a man whose posture was somewhat askew from years of slinking and bobbing his way through the battlefield of public opinion, but he could not be dissuaded, or so he said, from personally informing Herr Powenz of the news—which, though on the one hand was quite distressing, on the other hand was very good news indeed. To wit: a relative of the same name had passed away in America, but not before he had bequeathed his entire fortune, without exception,

223

to his beloved relatives in Moessel, that is, to whichever of them might survive him. "Signed, sealed and delivered in New Eastcheap, California," Dattel concluded. "May I be the first to extend my congratulations." Powenz received these words with proud composure.

It was only a sort of preliminary notification, and the extent of what was assumed to be a fabulous fortune was not given, nor was it revealed just what sort of place this New Eastcheap might be. (Truth to tell, it was a small gold-rush town built of corrugated iron and tin cans, and its sheriff proved, on closer inspection, to be a highly disreputable character and a bosom buddy of Uncle Melchior.) Nevertheless that very same day everyone in Moessel knew that that lucky son of a gun Powenz had become a real millionaire overnight!

How the Moesselers did rejoice!

"Well, that does it," Frau Quiebus cried when she heard the incredible news. "But, God willing, it won't last long. People like that simply don't know how to handle money."

In a malicious letter to the editor, Baltus Powenz expressed his gratitude for the countless expressions of friendship that, to his great surprise, he had received upon the occasion of a slight betterment in his fortunes. Though not in a position to fulfill all the hundreds of requests that had come his way, he found it incumbent upon him to announce publicly how useful such suggestions had been in convincing him that, after these many long years of penury, he ought to put these well-deserved riches to charitable use. And first and foremost, he considered his obligations to his new homeland to be by far the most pressing.

"So, now he's off to America," they all said. "He's leaving Moessel and the money's going with him." There seemed to be no other explanation for Powenz's words.

Shortly thereafter, the business community likewise wrote a letter to the editor. In florid prose they described Moessel's desperate financial situation and asserted that the intolerance of town officials was encouraging the exodus of capital. Immediate corrective measures were required, for the golden pedestal on which the town's welfare stood was the purchasing power of the general public!

Violent attacks were directed above all against Knipfel and Gockeley, whose shortsightedness and unenlightened views were bringing about the depopulation and ruin of Moessel—for people now recalled only too well just how seriously they had offended Powenz by rejecting his petition for a building permit.

The poor mayor had simply no other choice. In the name of the entire population of Moessel, he would have to beg Powenz—suddenly a very valuable citizen—to remain in their midst. One must always keep one's feet firmly planted in the facts, he declared. Besides which, the Powenzes were basically quite splendid folks; they were overgrown children, children of nature. A deputation betook itself to the Elephant House.

"Stay here among us, dear Herr Powenz," Dattel exclaimed warmly at the close of his speech. "Stay here in Moessel and live on the lean of the land!"

He had, moreover, brought along the approval for Powenz's building permit, the one which at one time had unfortunately been refused on account of a grievous oversight. And in reparation, one might say (and Dattel said it with a certain whimsy), the city was giving him the lot located directly across from Frau Quiebus's house.

Dressed as always in his formal coat, wearing no collar and with only his greasy ivory collar button beneath his adam's apple, Powenz dabbed at his decidedly dry eyes with a red handkerchief, gratefully accepted the gift with a voice barely able to suppress a sob and drank a toast to the town. With justifiable pride he then showed these rare guests to his home his collection of bricks, and they all left the house exuding confidence. And Powenz already had a well-healed buyer for the lot the city had given him.

Chapter Nine

Begins with Well and ends with a period

Well, Powenz did not go to America. Not too long before all this, the town of Moessel had sold to the small neighboring village of Kyps—and at a price the town council thought exceptionally good —both that small idyllic island with its beach popularly known as Powenz Island and the so-called Powder Woods bordering on it, also known as Paradise, a tract of land about which probably more anecdotes were told than about any other in the area. It was, after all, a fertile garden of love, famous for its strawberries, blueberries, bilberries and brambleberries. It was such a charming bit of landscape that Baedeker's guidebook describes it as well worth a visit.

This fabled tract was now part and parcel of Kyps, and for it Powenz traded in the lot the town had given him free. This then was his "magic spot," lying right under the town's nose, but now unfortunately no longer within its taxable territory.

There on the edge of the woods, just across from the historic, silver-gray beach, was where

Baltus Powenz planned to put down his roots at last.

The amazed citizenry were first made aware of all this by a large, neatly lettered sign proclaiming that here a new one-family house was to be built for the Powenzes, that Baltus Powenz was architect, contractor and construction supervisor, and that trespassing by unauthorized persons was strictly forbidden. The overly curious were driven off by Jubal, a smart-alecky kid by this time, who went around carrying a collection box, the proceeds of which were ostensibly for the construction of a Chapel of the Seven Sleepers.

Public interest in the erection of the Powenz house was lively beyond all expectation. There was always an audience, and the Powenzes enjoyed every minute of it.

Heinrich stayed away as long as the cellar was being dug out (for, of course, a roomy wine cellar was included in the plans).

"It hurts me so," he said darkly. "Oh, brothers, you know, all that senseless wounding of the earth and..."

He simply could not watch, and he would most certainly have only been in the way, rescuing a dung beetle here and a grub there, constantly striving to reunite the two halves of a bisected worm or to transport the wounded back to his curious animal hospital in an attempt to save them. There, under his tender yet vigorous care, many a poor snail with a crushed house, many a half-frozen bumblebee, many a bruised frog had already fully recuperated. Granted, one sparrow that he had nursed back to health was unfortunately devoured by a convalescing kitten.

But it was truly a delight to see how the other Powenzes went to work, tossing clumps of heavy earth or rusty yellow sand into the air with flashing silver spades. They were all tanned a glorious brown, and there was an aura of sunlight about their perspiring bodies. Mother Sabina and Lilith brought their meals out to them.

With the very first thrust of the spade a gushing spring flowed up toward them like a greeting from the earth, providing them with their own source of water. And on the second day this busy family of diggers unexpectedly hit upon two rusty helmets and two breastplates, evidently from the days of the Thirty Years' War. Overjoyed at their find, they picked up the armor, and the bones of two dead knights rattled inside—presumably soldiers shot during a fracas and interred here by their brothers-in-arms. At the formal laying of the cornerstone, a zinc box was bricked into the wall; before soldering it shut, they placed in it a silver coin found with the armor and bearing the likeness of Kaiser Ferdinand, several coins then in circulation, the newspapers of all political parties

229

(which meant a lot of paper!), a current map of the town and a brief history of the rise of Powenz House (entitled *The Powenzarium*).

The cellar was not yet fully excavated when the will that promised to make them all rich arrived. Accompanied by Councilman Gockeley, a man learned in the law, Mayor Dattel took the trouble of personally appearing in good Powenz's apartment in order to proceed with the opening of the "testamentary disposition," as he put it. He had not omitted to bring a bouquet for the lady of the house. Sabina accepted it, deeply touched. It was, she said, the first time in her life that someone had brought her flowers.

Under the terms of the will, Baltus Powenz was appointed sole heir to his brother Melchior, who had long ago disappeared while pursuing mammon in America. The younger Powenzes responded with an earsplitting Indian whoop; but that sound soon dwindled to a whine when, amidst all the high-flown prose, there emerged the indubitable fact that this was not a matter of an inherited fortune but of "obligations." To be sure, millions were involved—but of debts and debts alone.

It grew very quiet in the room. Herr Gockeley giggled. Nor could Dattel hide the malicious joy he felt, though he dutifully pointed out that Powenz could, of course, refuse the inheritance, which he most earnestly urged him to do. Quite apart from that, however, he presumed that in the wake of this startling turn of events, the family would hardly feel the need to remain within Moessel's walls.

For the first time ever, old Baltus seemed to lose his composure. His grief was obvious. He was a broken man.

His sons drew long faces. They balled their fists. Lilith stroked her father's hair.

Only Fabian, who while the will was being read had for once not fallen asleep, seemed unperturbed. He turned to his father with a smile and whispered something in his ear. And lo! Baltus's face brightened. He nodded eagerly.

"What would we do without you, Fabi," he said and shook his hand.

"Would you please be so kind," Dattel impatiently interjected, "as to give your mayor an answer. I ask you, Powenz, do you accept the inheritance or not?"

Baltus stood up, his face bright as the sun. And though Sabina pleaded, "Don't do it, Powenz, I beg you!" and though Kaspar rolled up his sleeves and made ready to bounce these bums, these stooges with rear ends for faces (he meant Messrs. Dattel and Gockeley), and though Jadup and Zephirin pointed out that they still had the lot, the bricks and their own bare hands to work with,

Powenz declared that under the present circumstances he saw no alternative but to accept the inheritance.

Dattel and Gockeley looked at each other in bewilderment. He did not think he had heard correctly, the mayor wheezed. Powenz really must be reasonable. They were only considering his best interests. But Powenz stood firm.

"I accept, Dattel. Period."

He opened the door for them, and the gentlemen departed.

Fabian was quite right, of course. Mounds of debts are also a kind of capital. Creditors don't like to lose everything, either. Powenz even succeeded in wangling a loan out of them to pay for future enterprises.

The next day the cornerstone was laid. As a matter of courtesy, the entire town council was invited to the ceremony (who just as courteously declined the honor). Nevertheless, such a large crowd appeared that the well-stocked hot dog and beer concession (run by Frau Powenz with Jubal's help) turned a tidy profit.

Among those in attendance, by the way, were astonishing numbers of children with Powenz faces. And although not all of them bore that proud name, their father greeted them with affectionate words and the admonition to be worthy of the family name; to be, that is, fearless, festive and fertile.

Those three words rang like a hammer on an anvil, echoing across the woodlands. In a spontaneous burst of enthusiasm three cheers went up for Baltus, who was deeply moved. Caps flew into the air, Fabian beat his bass drum and Jadup his snare in a flourish so loud it could be heard all over town—though, one must presume, with mixed feelings. Afterwards there was dancing to the music of the Powenz band, and that night the gala festivities were ended with a traditional display of fireworks. It was unanimously decided to repeat the celebration each year on the same date—June 19.

For the raising of the walls, the numbered bricks were transported by garlanded teams of horses with many giddaps and whoas. Heinrich, however, proved especially inept at bricklaying. He took ever so long to decide which of the many identical bricks he should pick up first—they were all so alike—and when after extended consideration he finally picked one up, he would have his doubts again and put it back down, grab a second, then a third, discard them both, reconsider and try once more with the first and shake his head while turning it over and over, undecided whether it might not work best the other way around or whether he should perhaps put the bottom on top or vice versa. Finally, with a sad smile, he would put it back with the others and try his luck all over again. His father, too, though laying bricks at a furious pace, would sometimes pause in his work to read the number on a brick and remember. "And now lie there, cheek to cheek," he whispered with deep emotion, setting one brick beside the other.

Not everyone worked at once. Usually they would alternate so that two of them could provide music for the others.

They had, moreover, left four pine trees standing, using them as live poles for their scaffolding, for in that part of the country tree trunks are usually bare except for their small murmuring crowns.

The house's new, improved ground plan formed a rectangle just as it had in the original plan that Herr Knipfel had thought was best described as a "box." No wonder, then, that an article now appeared in the *Moessel Courier* that spoke of how "ne-er-do-wells were vandalizing the local countryside" and implied that lovers of art should not permit a thing like this to happen but, rather, even at this late date lodge a vigorous protest. This foolish attack failed miserably and was parried by an article in a prominent regional newspaper. In it

Knipfel's buildings were amusingly and graphically compared to the historical originals from which they had been adapted. Written by Zephirin, this essay spoke openly of Knipfel's well-known talents as a tracer and copyist. It was greeted with a storm of approval by younger architects.

Soon thereafter, Knipfel, sorely offended, retired to private life.

Chapter Ten

Is especially for lovers of blueberry pie

The Powenz house grew.

One could already recognize the rooms of father Powenz's future laboratory, Zephirin's artist's studio, and, on the ground floor, Fabian's sacred sleeping quarters. These were so cleverly planned that everything was built to be within reach of the couch. In a recent publication, that great hypnosopher has included for the first time informative illustrations of the Fabianist Patented Bed, as well as the totally soundproof cultic sleeping room. And it represents as well the first public showing of his patented machine for falling asleep: a cradle, driven by electricity to the accompaniment of a monotonous bass-drum beat that Fabian himself composed. In an appendix to this remarkable book, the author has included an excellent bibliography of books to fall asleep by, where along with many other contemporary titles, the good-natured author's own books are also to be found. Though its many suggestions have a sound basis in nature and have all been tested by the author

236

himself, the book is, I grant, somewhat tiresome. It is titled *Falling Asleep Quickly and Easily.*

There was also an inventor's workshop, where they hoped to work together to build an automobile that would replace the annoying noise of the motor with dulcet pipe-organ music, and after that an umbrella-airplane (to be folded up and carried under the arm), the designs for which were already finished.

Out of a fine sensitivity for Heinrich's personality, they had made provision for a small animal clinic in the woods nearby. It was to be the home of the lovely cow Madeleine, she of the great silky copper-colored ears, as well as that of his pet raven and of whatever other creatures he might be keeping at the moment.

How often I watched with silent satisfaction as father Powenz built! His illustrated torso bared, his red face wreathed almost totally in his great white beard—a magnificent, unforgettable sight. In those hands bricks looked like dominoes. He built, and his splendid sons assisted. He built and sang—it was a delight simply to watch!

At last Heinrich proved good for something—preparing the mortar. He mixed it cautiously and was careful to keep any flies from drowning in it.

If the night was a fine one, they would work by lantern light, and sometimes the friends and the natural sons of Baltus and Kaspar would come and volunteer to help a little.

Fabian had never been awake as much as he was then. And little Jubal, all covered with lime, proved very useful for all sorts of fetching and carrying.

There was great joy and excitement the day the grateful children of Kyps arrived in solemn procession, bearing the generous gift of a dozen large blueberry pies topped with powdered sugar (each pie plate borne on four youthful shoulders); at their head was Baptist, a lad of Powenzian blood who was already a dependable leader of men. One of the pies was, sadly, no longer in edible condition, having suffered considerable damage during an insidious attack by some Moessel riffraff, who were, however, successfully repulsed.

This joyous Parade of the Blueberry Pies is also repeated now every year, and, so I hear, is growing more and more festive. The finest and largest pie is awarded a prize. From near and far happy little children arrive in white frocks embroidered with flowers, just so they can return home that evening stained blue and howling loudly. The mayor personally reviews the Pie Parade as it marches by.

Which proves that now and then it is the peaceable Powenzian spirit and Powenzian mores that carry the day.

Chapter Eleven

*Begins very sadly, but ends with splendid
prospects for the future*

Shortly after construction began, it became clear that Heinrich was not at all well. He froze in summer and winter alike, despite heavy clothing; his face was an ashen white. While in the hospital for observation for a few days, he became acquainted with a delicate girl who was afflicted with the same ominous symptoms. Both were soon released.

Heinrich and Friederika were very much in love. Following the sun, they would walk together, always shivering and incapable of warming one another. Their blood grew thinner and colder from day to day.

But when they would sit all bundled up on the sunniest bench on Tunnel Mountain, snuggled together in the quiet warmth of the afternoon and breathing shallowly, then Heinrich's eyes would suddenly grow very large and very dull. For then he saw (o how very strange!) the peaceful little town of Moessel lying in ruins, saw how the church steeples no longer stood like pious, stony-helmeted watchmen, but suddenly shattered, how houses, row upon row, collapsed. He saw the fire leap high, devouring the woodlands like a gigantic red cow, and he heard the dreadful bells of terror and the keening of widows.

"What's wrong with you?" Friederika asked, for she saw nothing of all this.

"Oh God," said Heinrich; but then he considered a moment and gave a little cough. "Let's go, it's getting cool."

Friederika knew that Heinrich was forever seeing ghastly eventualities everywhere about him—a tree struck by lightning, stars falling from the heavens, a child exposed to constant mortal danger.

Both the lovers had complexions much like bluish milk, and when their chilly mouths met to kiss, their hearts were only barely set atremble. Plagued by shivers and nosebleeds, they sat next to one another every day on the warmest bench they could find. It was their little consolation that their noses bled at the same time.

Now, one would certainly think that they would also have both died at the same time. But they could not manage it. Friederika died first and Heinrich had to do it all alone.

And although she had been ever so delicate

and transparent in her last days, there were enough earthly remains of her that Heinrich shuddered when he gazed upon them.

But by a seemingly improbable accident, it fell to him—to gentle, foolish Heinrich, whose tender kindness and soulful decency had been met by the Powenz family with what was for them unusual patience, almost reverence—that he was able to ensure the economic future of his loved ones for what we humans like to think of as forever.

Gentle Heinrich loved animals more than people—we know that. We also know that his friendship with Madeleine the heifer, whom he had brought back from the battlefront, sometimes served as the occasion for some rather crude jokes on the part of his mischievous brothers. His animal clinic was amazingly successful, a fact that did not go unnoticed. Kaspar had accidentally run over a puppy with his bike and crippled both its back legs. Heinrich rigged up a little wagon to which its immobile hindparts could be fastened, and the puppy merrily went for walks on its forelegs while taking its rear for a ride. A lizard that had lost its tail out of pure fright grew back three new ones at once under Heinrich's tender care. A grasshopper that he had found half-crushed at the side of the road recovered completely, setting new jumping records. And even Heinrich himself seemed to be getting better since he had begun more and more to devote himself to sick insects, squirrels, hedgehogs and birds.

He also knew the reason for these miraculous recoveries. But it was only after his all too early demise that it became generally known. From earliest childhood, Heinrich had liked to busy himself with composing last wills and testaments, and his anxious concern not to offend anyone meant that each will was quickly discarded in favor of a new one. After his death, a highly detailed document was discovered, from which it became apparent that the water that had bubbled up during the excavation of the cellar was in fact a mineral spring. He had been watering his animals with it and had sent some off for analysis to Professor Schlegelmilch, who found it to contain the highest percentage of radium of any spring water in all Germany. The will, written in Heinrich's own small, neat hand, ended with the request of the testator that, should his discovery ever yield a profit for his heirs, a considerable sum be laid aside for the maintenance of the animal clinic he had founded. Which was then done.[15]

[15]Thus Bad Heinrichsbrunn by Kyps (owners: Powenz, Inc.) came into being (all other accounts are incorrect!). Though of recent origin, it is known worldwide and is heavily frequented, a place of healing for suffering mankind. For further information, write directly to the management.

News of this miraculous discovery had hardly got out before furious digging began in every yard and garden in Moessel. (I have never met anyone who did not immediately look at the ground if he saw someone else find a penny on the street— there just might be one there for him too.) At first it appeared that Gockeley's excavations were to be crowned with success, but unfortunately it turned out that he had merely broken into the town water main.

O poor Moessel, how you were deceived and how pitiable was your fate. For although Heinrich went to his eternal rest all too soon, his prophecies were fulfilled several thousand times over.

Chapter Twelve

The last one

In his *Contra Powenz*, Doctor Gottlieb Gilpin contends that all the actions of this family, described here with such relentless fidelity, were characterized by a "will to destruction," a contention to which I object most emphatically. I do not wish to deny that many deeds of the Powenzes were somewhat improper or vexatious, that some even came close to being criminal and wicked. But I must nevertheless concur with one of Baltus's maxims: what counts is sweet life itself and not the mere living of it.

To the great joy of all Powenzialists, this view of life found symbolic expression on an evening that may justly be called an historic occasion, marking as it did the completion of the house's frame, the so-called Raise the Roof Ceremony. For on that night all the Powenzes displayed their talents in a kind of family revue. With the aid of Zephirin's clever lighting, the scaffolding was skillfully adapted to create a new sort of stage for an impressive presentation of entertainments, all of them displaying not just skill but also talent and pure unadulterated artistry.

The large audience in attendance heartily applauded the parody entitled *Scaffold Gymnastics*, a breakneck satire of contemporary sports and of the current rage for establishing world records. They were equally pleased with Zephirin's speed-painting show, which included delightful caricatures of Moessel's most prominent citizens, and with Jadup's song with harp accompaniment (by Baltus Powenz). Of the same exceptional quality was Violand's sketch, *The Mute Magician*, where the sole accompaniment to his sorcery were his own witty, eloquent hand motions.

This event, which became known as the Powenz Festival, was spoken of for a long time thereafter.

Nor should one forget the exciting one-act play, *Skeletons in the Night*, a wild comedy replete with frenzied music, dance, murder, drunkenness and all kinds of love. In its own way, it was a pioneering work, for the set was simply overrun from top to bottom, upstairs and down, with acrobatic vitality, with color, light, music and poetry. For the finale, two rotating spotlights and various other magical special effects were used in the production of *The Haunted House*, a drama almost frightening in its effectiveness, for suddenly everything—woods and house, Powenz pack and audience—seemed to sway, to totter, to shrink, to grow, to be transformed, until finally the lights went out and the so-called Great Powenzian Laughing Song rose up from the entire assembly like an unearthly moan ascending into the clear starry night. All in all, a perfect evening!

When the audience had finally departed and I was about to say goodbye myself, Baltus Powenz held me back with a massive hand. Then, giving Jubal—who looked quite comical in an angel costume—the order to light our way with a torch, he asked whether he might show me the "inner house" (as he called it). I can still clearly recall how his voice trembled with emotion. He still wore royal garb from the last scene of the play; on his large head was a golden crown of paper. He was a bit tipsy, and though I was very tired I did not want to offend him, especially since he was usually very sensitive when in his cups. Nor did I regret going with him.

"If I were a rich man, I would buy a house," the old man said with a smile. This was a favorite citation of his, a paradigmatic sentence from an old grammar book; and I have since come to suspect that these simple words may well have given direction to his whole life.

I still can see the old man, the drunken king of the stage, standing there in his brick chamber, the air cool with the odor of mortar. He staggered a bit, but with dignity, and ever and again he said just one word with great fervor, "Splendid, splendid!"

Powenz showed me his future workshop, which he called a pyrotechnic laboratory, showed me Zephirin's studio for the mass production of kitsch paintings and, finally, Fabian's ingenious Chapel of Sleep, where he hoped to be able to reach everything while lying in his cultic bed. Only one picture was to be hung in the room: the Lord resting from his labors on the seventh day. Mother Sabina's one modest request had also been granted—parquet floors, to the care and maintenance of which she devoted the rest of her life. For parquet floors (in a light wood, if possible) are the pride of every housewife.

So we walked through the whole house, with Jubal the saucy angel lighting our way. Now and again Powenz would reach out his great hand to grasp mine, making it crack under the pressure, and draw me up very close to the masonry.

"There," he said, pointing at a brick, "that is number 977. I brought it home myself. I remember it as if it were today. It fell out of a cart and landed in the white dust of Kyps Road. And here, this one here I brought home from the war. It is part of the ruins of Ferme Trouchy. The whole house is constructed out of such stories. This one here was given me by a sweet young girl, as a token of gratitude. Her name was Isabella."

I noticed how hard he took it that all his beloved bricks would now be plastered over. After all, he knew each of them personally.

There are things about which one does not jest. That night I saw this old sinner, lost in reveries, stroke many a brick as he would a loved one's cheek, even kissing some of them. And I was touched.

That night remains unforgettable, and even today when I walk through those bright, neatly wallpapered rooms, I am often reminded how each of those wonderful bricks, though invisible now, passed through his mighty hands. And not long ago I saw—that is, if one of his fine sons was not playing another practical joke on me—the restless shade of Baltus Powenz himself staggering through these rooms, and I heard him mutter, laugh, sing and converse with his bricks.

Sad to say, he never had the pleasure of seeing his house completed.

Three days after these triumphant festivities, the eccentric old man met—I almost said, was favored by—his extraordinary death. And I view that fact as both a sign of punishment and of special grace.

And, dear reader, should you wish to know

Powenz Monument (by Bernauer)
Baltusplatz, Moessel on the Maar
(Kypsian marble)

the circumstances under which Baltus Powenz—down to his last hair and tooth, and, yes, with all his visions of the future and the dark moments of his past—was metamorphosed from a terrestrial into a celestial being by a catapult from heaven, then I must beg you to reread chapter one.

Addendum

Deals with the inner life of the Powenz pack

There are many who claim that Powenzes have no souls. They are incorrect, I believe, though when we speak of souls we generally speak of something invisible and rather difficult to imagine. Invisible? Not entirely, it seems to me; for sometimes "at divine moments its crystalline body flashes like a tear." Inaudible? Not really, for sometimes it can be heard in the words of unhappy mortals, of poets and sages—and so, to some extent, in the words of Powenzes as well. Theologically speaking, the subjects included in this little folder from the file of human nature (if I may so term the present volume) belong to those poor sinners at whom all of us are unfortunately only too ready to cast the first stone.

I am no moralist. I have no desire to whitewash the Powenzes. And nevertheless, I maintain that they do have souls—and ergo, a God.

Sometimes when I would happen upon them, especially when they would be enjoying the silver-gray beach along the Maar River, all of them clad only in a natural tan (the state, that is, in which they were originally intended to be), I would get the delightful feeling that they were animals, or creatures very closely related to animals. By which I mean no disparagement—quite the opposite. When I think of wild Baltus and his reddish hide, when I recall the pictures that adorned his massive body like strange symbols of life, like inscriptions of heaven and earth upon the walls of a temple, I am reminded of the God who abides within animals. We know that of their own free will, this remarkable man's sons asked their Uncle Melchior, an adept in the ancient art of tattooing, to do to them what had been done to their father. Thus we find Kaspar's muscular body ornamented with charming scenes from the immortal legend of Cupid and Psyche. Heinrich's thin white skin was decorated with an animal paradise, while Fabian was a walking mathematics textbook, one that professed his admiration for famous formulae (the Pythagorean theorem, for instance) as well as for themes from his favorite sonatas, all of them displayed to the world in tattoo blue. Jadup's lovely body was left unmarked, nor did Lilith wish to be so adorned. Zephirin, however, artist that he was, learned this fine art from his uncle. He not only practices it, but he will also see to it that it is handed on, until that day comes at last when nature, by force of habit or memory, produces what so far we have been able to inoculate only by careful, tedious needlework—the illustrated man.

An old medieval proverb says, "Each human breast should have its window." Let us gaze within our Baltus's tufted breast. And what do we see? The heart of a child! Verily—for it is a heart filled with thoughts of toys and games. But what of Kaspar, so often slandered and so often loved? I have never known a single one of the women who were so very close to him to say anything untoward about him!

They all called him a fine young man. "You simply *have* to like him," they said. And his soul? He bore it unmarred within a heart that ever rejoiced in love. In his own way, he had made a great many people abundantly happy in the way they wanted.

Granted, I can offer no proof of my soul, or of yours, or of the Powenzes, dear reader. I can only try to make its existence credible. Most assuredly, people cannot be called wicked who were so capable of loving and of being loved as were these irrepressible and highly unruly friends of ours. It may be objected that not all of the Powenzes were so natural, so rife with comedy as I claim. Many may say, for example, that Jadup was abnormal or degenerate. Well, degeneration is not the exclusive privilege of better families. It is also known among primitive tribes. It is, in fact, nature's defense mechanism for preventing the world from grow-

The Cave Powenz
Powenz primigenus
Reconstruction of a cave mural
in the Powenz Museum

ing all too normal. "All great things are abnormal, and the everyday is the enemy of the wonderful," is Karl Butter's song.

A renowned psychologist once called the Powenz pack both coarse and passionate. They were, he said, typical representatives of our epoch, barbaric and heathen creatures that characterize the early phase of our era of words, tin, rubber and air. They are those indestructible personalities that God so happily utilizes whenever he wants to vex the world—and to bless it. For a divinity dwells within them.

It would appear, then, that they are the heralds of a new race, a race that, without prejudice and free of the cares of an outworn civilization, becomes the agar-agar for a new culture, a race that is perhaps susceptible to the flames of a new religion!

Powenz Family Tree

Progenitors:

Adam Powenz ∞ Eva, née Ribby

(not fully researched)

|

Cave Powenz (c. 5000 B.C.)

|

B. Poventius Mosselinus, soldier (c. 80 A.D.)

|

Wenzel Pohwentz, peasant (c. 1300)

|

Sir Utz Pohwentz, robber-knight †1499

|

Hanske Powentz †1546
sailor

|

John Powens	Pierre Povence	Po-weng-si	Fabulus Powenz
(Eng. line)	(Fr. line)	(Chin. line)	†1601 piper
Lord Powens	Maurice Povence	?	Florin Powenz
*1892	*1902 actor		†1645 potter

Till Powenz
†1703 puppeteer

|

Karsten Powenz
†1730
alchemist

|

Dominikus Powenz
†1772
knife-grinder

|

Nikolo Powenz (aka Povencini)
highwire artist

Hokus Powenz †1801
magician

|

August Powenz (aka Powo) †1839
clown

|

Quirin Powenz †1839 ∞ Resi Dubbergast †?
harpist and bard

|

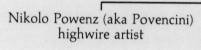

Hieronymus Powenz
*1860 †1924
world-traveler

Baltus Powenz ∞ Sabina Schwampus
*1864 †1929

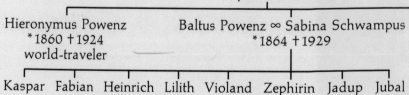

Kaspar Fabian Heinrich Lilith Violand Zephirin Jadup Jubal